CATALAN IN THREE MONTHS

D1354607

Hugo's Simplified System

Catalan in
Three Months

Stuart C. Poole

Hugo's Language Books Limited

Written by

Stuart C. Poole

Centre for Continuing Education,
The University of Edinburgh

Cover photo (Robert Harding Picture Library):
La Sagrada Família, Barcelona

Set in 10/12 Plantin by
Keyset Composition, Colchester
Printed and bound in Great Britain by
Page Brothers, Norwich

Preface

Benvinguts –

Have you ever studied Spanish before a visit to Barcelona, the Costa Brava or Majorca, only to be confronted with such strange words as **benvinguts** as soon as you get off the plane?

If so, that is because the north-east of Spain has a widely spoken language of its own, Catalan, as well as Spanish.

The territory in which Catalan was spoken expanded in the Middle Ages, not least when the ruler Jaume el Conqueridor pushed back the Arabs in the thirteenth century, and the language is now spoken from Andorra to the Balearic Islands, from Perpignan in France to Valencia.

This despite the fact that Catalan has often been suppressed by Spanish rulers, most recently by Franco. But it has always been too robust to be wiped out and it now stands as an official language in the north-east alongside Spanish. It is spoken by more people than some national languages such as Danish.

Being spoken in what was once part of the Roman empire, Catalan is derived from Latin. Students acquainted with either French or Spanish will have an advantage when learning Catalan as it is something of a cross between these two languages. As an example, a small house is referred to as a **casa petita**. Underground trains in Barcelona ask intending passengers to allow alighting passengers to get off, the Catalan text above the doors, **Deixeu sortir**, reflecting the Spanish verb 'dejar' and the French verb 'sortir'.

Contents

Pronunciation

This section refers to some of the principal features of Catalan pronunciation. Further assistance will be given in the first three lessons by imitated pronunciation, enabling you to get to grips with the Catalan sounds. Those of you with the cassettes, however, will be able to imitate the pronunciation more closely.

In Catalan the stress usually falls on the last vowel that is followed by another letter:

la casa petita   the small house
(ler 'kahz-er'per- tee-ter)
el meu amic   my friend
(erl 'may-oo er-'meek)

When, however, the word ends in **s** the stress falls wherever it would have fallen without that **s**, thus avoiding the stress being altered in the plural form of words:

les cases petites   the small houses
(lers 'kahz-ers per-'tee-ters)

Where the stressed vowel does not comply with the above rules this is indicated in the spelling by the use of an accent mark over the stressed vowel:

plànol ('pler-nol)   town plan
català (ker-ter-'lah)   Catalan
església (ez-'glay-zee-er)   church
anglès (ern-'gless)   English
jardí (jar-'dee)   garden
autobús (ah'oo-to-'boos)   bus

The vowel **a** always takes the grave accent (**à**). The vowels **i** and **u** always take the acute accent (**í, ú**). The vowels **e** and **o** can take either accent, depending on how they are pronounced. A stressed **e** may be either 'open' as in English 'get' or 'closed' as in English

9

'grey'. In **cafè** ('coffee') the **e** is open, while in **església** it is closed. As these examples show, the accent mark when required reflects the difference in sound.

Similarly, a stressed **o** may be open, as in English 'got', or closed, as in English 'goat'. In **dona** ('woman') the **o** is open, in **habitació** ('room') it is closed.

Stressed vowels are more distinct than unstressed vowels. Thus the first vowel of **casa**, the stressed one, is like the first vowel of the English word 'hazard', while the second vowel, the unstressed one, is also similar in each word.

The weakness of an unstressed **a** is such that it is generally indistinguishable from an unstressed **e**. Thus, while a final **a** becomes **e** in the plural, the sound remains the same:

la casa petita
les cases petites

The four definite articles (**el**, **la**, **els**, **les**), the equivalents of 'the', all have this weak sound and so are much less distinct than their Spanish equivalents.

Similarly, an unstressed **o** is weaker than a stressed **o**, the former being indistinguishable from an unstressed **u**. Thus the first vowels of **professor** (proo-fess-'or) and **universitat** (oony-versy-'tat) have the same sound.

In our imitated pronunciation we use *er* to indicate the weak **a** and **e** – see the note on page 13. We should also explain that the **au** combination is imitated as ah'oo; although it sounds roughly like the 'ow' in 'cow', there's a bit more of an 'oo' at the end. (Had we put 'blow' for **blau**, you could have been confused. Bear in mind that the imitated system is only approximate, and buy the audio cassettes that are an optional extra to this book.)

The letter **x** may produce a similar sound to the combination 'sh' in English. Thus the Catalan combination **tx** produces the sound that is represented in English by 'ch', as does **g** after an **i**:

el cotxe del senyor Puig   Mr. Puig's car
(erl 'kotch-er derl sern-'yo pooch)

Between vowels a single **s** is voiced, that is it requires the vibration of the vocal cords, as in the English word 'has'. The unvoiced sound, as in the English word 'sad', is represented by double **s** between vowels. As in English, this latter sound may also be represented by **c** before **e** or **i**:

les cases del passeig de Gràcia
the houses of the Passeig de Gràcia
(le*r*s ′kahz-e*r*s de*r*l pe*r*-′setch de*r* ′gras-y-e*r*)

As in French, the use of a cedilla allows the letter **c** to produce this sound before the vowels **a**, **o** and **u** as well:

la plaça the square
(le*r* ′pla-se*r*)

The letter **j** may be pronounced as in French or as in English. The letter **g** is pronounced in the same way when it is followed by the vowels **e** or **i**:

el jardí del meu germà my brother's garden
(e*r*l jar-′dee de*r*l ′may-oo jer-
′mah)

Like Spanish, Catalan has the letter **ll** which is pronounced like the 'lli' in the English word 'million'. Catalan also has a double **l** which is distinguished by a dot:

un fill intel.ligent an intelligent son
(oon ′fil-ye*r* intelli-′gen)

The letter **h** is silent. A final **t** is silent after **l** or **n**:

un home molt intel.ligent a very intelligent man
(oon ′o-me*r* mol intelli-′gen)

A final **r** is often silent. It is silent at the end of an infinitive.

A sound may be influenced by an adjoining sound. In the word **escola** ('school') the **s** is unvoiced like the **c** that follows, while in **església** ('church') the voiced **g** is preceded by a voiced **s**. This applies even when the sounds are in different words; thus the **s** of **les** is unvoiced in **les cases** ('the houses') but voiced in **les dones** ('the women'). In **les esglésies** the **s** of **les** is voiced because it lies between two vowels.

Lesson 1

1 Gender

Nouns (words referring to objects, etc.) belong to one of two genders: masculine and feminine. It may help the student – who has probably already learnt some Spanish – to know that the gender of a Catalan word is usually the same as the gender of its Spanish equivalent.

A word is usually feminine if it ends with **a**: e.g. **dona** ('woman'), **església** ('church'). There are a few exceptions such as **mapa** ('map') and **dia** ('day'), these being masculine.

Other indications of feminine gender are the endings **-tat**, e.g. **ciutat** ('city', 'town'), and **-ció**, e.g. **habitació** ('room').

IMITATED PRONUNCIATION (1): 'don-er; ez-'glay-zee-er; 'mah-per; 'dee-er; see-oo-'tat; abby-tas-'yo.

2 Indefinite articles

For nouns of masculine gender the indefinite article, the equivalent of 'a' or 'an', is **un**. For nouns of feminine gender it is **una**, e.g.:

un barri	a district, quarter
un home	a man
una dona	a woman
una ciutat	a city, town

IMITATED PRONUNCIATION (2): oon; 'oo-ner; oon 'barry; oon 'o-mer; 'oo-ner 'don-er; 'oo-ner see-oo-'tat.

3 Definite article

For nouns of masculine gender the definite article, the equivalent of 'the', is **el**. For nouns of feminine gender it is **la**, e.g.:

el barri	the district, quarter
la dona	the woman
la ciutat	the city, town

Are you wondering why 'the man' has disappeared from the list above? Read on. Where words begin with a vowel sound the definite article is generally **l'**, e.g. **l'església** ('the church'). As the Catalan letter **h** is silent, this also applies to words which begin with **h**, e.g. **l'home** ('the man'), **l'habitació** ('the room').

The vowel of **la** is, however, retained before unstressed **(h)i** and **(h)u**, e.g. **la universitat** ('the university').

Remember what we said about the definite articles' vowel sounds being much weaker than in Spanish [page 10]. When reading the imitated pronunciation, take care not to sound the italic *r* which is so placed to indicate a weak vowel. For example, **l'home** is imitated as 'lo-me*r*: say the English word 'loam' and linger on the final sound, but don't let it become 'loamer'. The italic *r* also draws you away from sounding this particular word as 'lo-me or 'loamy'.

IMITATED PRONUNCIATION (3): e*r*l; le*r*; e*r*l 'barry; le*r* 'don-e*r*; le*r* see-oo-'tat; lez-'glay-zee-e*r*; 'lo-me*r*; labby-tas-'yo; le*r* oony-versy-'tat.

4 Use of the articles

The use of the articles sometimes differs from usage in English. Catalan may use an article where English does not. When referring to a category of object in general, for example, Catalan uses the definite article; while we talk about 'wine', Catalans talk about **el vi**.

Conversely, English may use an article where Catalan does not. This is the case, for example, when reference is made to somebody's profession:

L'home és professor.	The man is a teacher.

IMITATED PRONUNCIATION (4): 'lo-me*r* ays proo-fess-'or.

5 Adjectives

a) Adjectives usually follow the noun that they describe:

un barri vell	an old district
el Barri Gòtic	the Gothic Quarter
un home català	a Catalan man

But, for example, **bo** ('good') can be used before the noun, in which case the masculine singular form becomes **bon**:

bon dia	good day

IMITATED PRONUNCIATION (5a): oon 'barry 'bel-yer; erl 'barry 'go-tick; oon 'o-mer ker-ter-'lah; boh; bon; bon-'dee-er.

b) Certain adjectives which specify an object rather than describe it precede the noun:

el primer carrer	the first street
aquest carrer	this street

A few adjectives have different meanings depending on whether they come before or after the noun that they describe. Thus, for example, **pobre** indicates sympathy when placed before a noun and lack of money when placed after it:

Pobre home!	Poor man!
un home pobre	a poor man

IMITATED PRONUNCIATION (5b): erl pri-'may ker-'ray; er-'ket ker-'ray; 'po-brer 'o-mer; 'o-mer 'po-brer.

c) If the noun is feminine the adjective usually adopts a separate feminine form. This is often done simply by adding **a** to the end:

un home vell	an old man
una dona vella	an old woman

Any suppressed final **n** is reinstated in the feminine form:

un home català	a Catalan man
una dona catalana	a Catalan woman

An unvoiced final consonant may be replaced by its voiced equivalent in the feminine form:

un cotxe groc	a yellow car
una casa groga	a yellow house

A final **u** is replaced by **v**:

un cotxe blau	a blue car
una casa blava	a blue house

IMITATED PRONUNCIATION (5c): oon 'o-mer 'bel-yer; 'oo-ner 'don-er 'bel-yer; oon 'o-mer ker-ter-'lah; 'oo-ner 'don-er ker-ter-'lah-ner; oon 'kotch-er grock; 'oo-ner 'kahz-er 'grog-er; oon 'kotch-er blah'oo; 'oo-ner 'kahz-er 'blah-ver.

d) Many adjectives do not have a separate feminine form, examples being those that end in **-al**, **-ant** and **-il**:

la ciutat principal	the principal city
una obra important	an important work
la guerra civil	the civil war

The adjective **gran** ('big', 'large') is also invariable:

una gran casa	a large house

Some adjectives that end in **-e** replace the e by **-a** in the feminine, others do not:

	una dona pobra	a poor woman
But	**una dona jove**	a young woman

A noun may be omitted, leaving the article and the adjective to refer to an item if it has already been established what the item is:

el mapa català	the Catalan map
el català	the Catalan one

IMITATED PRONUNCIATION (5d): ler see-oo-'tat prin-se-'pahl; 'oo-ner 'ob-rer im-poor-'tan; ler 'gair-rer si-'veel; 'oo-ner gran 'kahz-er; 'oo-ner 'don-er 'pob-rer; 'oo-ner 'don-er 'jo-ver; erl 'mah-per ker-ter-'lah; erl ker-ter-'lah.

Vocabulary 1

In these lists, all Catalan nouns are preceded by the appropriate definite article (**el** for masculine, **la** for feminine); when the gender isn't obvious (**l'**) we follow the noun with *m* or *f*.

The vocabularies contain words you should already have come across in the lesson as well as others you'll need when working through the exercise that follows. Learn them all; test yourself by covering up first one column and then the other.

aquell	that
aquest	this
el barri	district, quarter
blanc	white
blau	blue
bo	good
brau	wild, rugged
el carrer	street
la casa	house
català	Catalan
la ciutat	city, town
civil	civil
la costa	coast
el cotxe	car
el dia	day
la dona	woman; wife
és	is
l'església (*f*)	church
gòtic	Gothic
gran	big, large, great
groc	yellow
la guerra	war
l'habitació (*f*)	room
l'home (*m*)	man
important	important
jove	young
el mapa	map
l'obra (*f*)	work
pobre	poor
primer	first
principal	principal
el professor	teacher (*m*)
la professora	teacher (*f*)

ric	rich
la universitat	university
vell	old
el vi	wine

IMITATED PRONUNCIATION: er-'kel-yer; er-'ket; 'barry; blanc; blah'oo; bo; brah'oo; ker-'ray; ker-ter-'lah; see-oo-'tat; si-'veel; 'koster; 'kotch-er; 'dee-er; 'don-er; ays; ez-'glay-zee-er; 'go-tick; gran; grock; 'gair-rer; abby-tas-'yo; 'o-mer; im-poor-'tan; 'jo-ver; 'mah-per; 'o-brer; 'po-brer; pri-'may; prin-se-'pahl; proo-fess-'or; proo-fess-'or-er; reek; oony-versy-'tat; 'bel-yer; bee.

Exercise 1

Give the Catalan for:

1 An old man
2 A rich woman
3 A young woman
4 A Catalan man
5 A Catalan town
6 The old quarter
7 The old church
8 That yellow house
9 The first house
10 This white house
11 White wine
12 The Wild Coast

When you have translated the above phrases, check them against the Catalan versions given in the Key towards the end of the book.

6 Subject pronouns

The subject pronouns, the equivalents of 'I', 'he', 'it' etc., are generally omitted:

L'home és ric.	The man is rich.
És molt ric.	He is very rich.

They tend to be used only to give emphasis, to avoid confusion or when no verb is used:

Ell és ric però ella és pobra.	He is rich but she is poor.

The subject pronouns are as follows:

jo	I	**nosaltres**	we
tu★	you	**vosaltres**★	you
vostè	you	**vostès**	you
ell	he, it	**ells**	they (*m*)
ella	she, it	**elles**	they (*f*)

★**Tu** is used when addressing somebody with whom you are on informal terms, such as a friend, and **vosaltres** when addressing two or more such people. Otherwise you should use **vostè** or **vostès**.

IMITATED PRONUNCIATION (6): 'lo-me*r* ays reek; ays mol reek; ell ays reek pe*r*-'roh 'ell-ye*r* ays 'pob-rer; jo; too; ell; 'ell-ye*r*; boos-'tay; noo-'zal-tress; boo-'zal-tress; e*r*lss; 'ell-e*r*s; boos-'tays.

7 Comparison

The comparative and superlative forms of the adjective are generally constructed using **més**:

L'home és ric.	The man is rich.
L'home és més ric que la dona.	The man is richer than the woman.
És l'home més ric de la ciutat.	He is the richest man in the town.

Just as English has some irregular forms such as 'better' and 'best', so Catalan has some irregular forms such as **millor**:

Aquest cotxe és millor.	This car is better.
Aquest cotxe és el millor.	This car is the best.

IMITATED PRONUNCIATION (7): mays; mil-'yo; e*r*-'ket; 'kotch-e*r*.

8 Fusion of prepositions and articles

The prepositions **a** ('to', 'at', 'in'), **de** ('of', 'from') and **per** ('by', 'through', 'for') fuse with the masculine definite article **el** and **els** as follows:

a + el = **al**	a + els = **als**
de + el = **del**	de + els = **dels**
per + el = **pel**	per + els = **pels**

al capdamunt del carrer	at the top of the street
el cotxe del fill	the son's car
gràcies pels mapes	thank you for the maps

IMITATED PRONUNCIATION (8): erl; erlss; derl; derlss; perl; perlss;
erl cap-der-'moon derl ker-'ray; erl 'kotch-er derl feel-'yer;
'grah-see-ers perlss 'mah-pers.

Vocabulary 2

a	to, at, in
el capdamunt	top
el capdavall	bottom
Catalunya	Catalonia
la catedral	cathedral
de	of, from
enllà	further
mes enllà de	beyond
esquerre	left
el fill	son
els fills	sons; children
la Generalitat	regional government of Catalonia
i	and
la mà	hand
més	more
millor	better; best
molt	much; very
on	where
el palau	palace
la part	part
per	by, through, for
però	but
la plaça	square
prop (de)	near (to)
reial	royal
xinès	Chinese

IMITATED PRONUNCIATION: er; cap-der-'moon; cap-der-'vall;
ker-ter-'loon-yer; ker-ter-'dral; der; en-'lya; mayz en-'lya der;
es-'kerr-er; 'feel-yer; 'feel-yers; jen-erally-'tat; ee; mah; mays;
mil-'yo; mol; on; per-'lah'oo; part; per-'roh; 'pla-ser; prop (der);
ray-'al; shi-'nays.

Social phrases 1

perdoni	excuse me
(moltes) gràcies (per)	thank you (very much) (for)
de res	don't mention it/you're welcome

IMITATED PRONUNCIATION: per-'donny; (molters) 'grah-see'ers (per); der ress.

Reading passage 1

After reading these passages you should try to answer the questions, before checking the answers, if possible.

Barcelona és la ciutat principal de Catalunya. El Barri Gòtic és més vell que el Barri Xinès. El Barri Gòtic és la part més vella de la ciutat. La catedral és al Barri Gòtic. La plaça de Catalunya és al capdamunt de la Rambla.

Answer the following questions. The answers are given in the Key at the end of the book.

1 Is the cathedral in the oldest part of the city?
2 Where is the Plaça de Catalunya?

Exercise 2

Give the Catalan for:

1 The old man's son is a teacher.
2 The teacher's house is at the bottom of the street.
3 It is yellow.
4 The teacher's car is white.
5 The old woman is richer than the teacher.
6 She is the richest woman in the town.
7 The old woman's house is in the square.
8 The house is white.
9 It is very big.
10 It is near the principal church.
11 The church is very old.
12 It is older than the palace.

CONVERSATION

*These conversations should be read aloud until you can read them
without hesitation, and the use of idioms, new vocabulary and
constructions should be noted.*

L'home	Perdoni. On és el Palau de la Generalitat? *Excuse me. Where is the Palau de la Generalitat?*
La dona	És al capdamunt del primer carrer, a la plaça de Sant Jaume. És a mà esquerra. *It is at the top of the first street, in the Plaça de Sant Jaume. It is on the left.*
L'home	I el Palau Reial Major? *And the Palau Reial Major?*
La dona	És més enllà, prop de la catedral. *It is further on, near to the cathedral.*
L'home	Moltes gràcies. *Thank you very much.*
La dona	De res. *You're welcome.*

Lesson 2

9 Plural

a) As in English, the plural form of nouns is indicated by an **s**. In the plural the definite article is **els** with masculine nouns and **les** with feminine nouns:

els homes	the men
les ciutats	the towns, cities

Nouns that end in **a** replace this final vowel by **es**:

les dones	the women

Where the plural **s** is added to a similarly sibilant sound **os** is added so that the plural ending remains distinct, just as, for example, 'bus' becomes 'buses' in English:

l'autobús	the bus	**els autobusos**	the buses
el mes	the month	**els mesos**	the months
el pis	the flat	**els pisos**	the flats
el despatx	the office	**els despatxos**	the offices

Other refinements include the reinstatement of final **n**:

l'habitació	the room	**les habitacions**	the rooms
la mà	the hand	**les mans**	the hands

IMITATED PRONUNCIATION (9a): erlz 'o-mers; lers see'oo-'tats; lerz 'don-ers; lah'oo-to-'booss; erlz ah'oo-to-'boo-zoss; erl mays; erlz 'may-zoos; erl peace; erlz 'pea-zoss; erl derss-'patch; erlz derss-'patch-ooss; lers abby-tas-'yons; ler mah; lerz mans.

b) Adjectives describing plural nouns also have to take a plural form. Adjectives form the plural in the same way that nouns do:

els barris vells	the old quarters
les dones velles	the old women
les dones catalanes	the Catalan women

The replacement of final **a** by **es** makes it necessary to amend the spelling on occasion in order to retain the sound of the preceding consonant:

l'amiga	the friend (*f*)	**les amigues**	the friends (*f*)
la plaça	the square	**les places**	the squares
rica	rich (*f*)	**riques**	rich (*f*)

IMITATED PRONUNCIATION (9b): erlz 'barryz 'bel-yers; lers 'don-ers 'bel-yers; lers 'don-ers ker-ter-'lah-ners; lah-'mee-ger; lerz ah-'mee-gers; ler 'pla-ser; lers 'pla-sers; 'ree-ker; 'reek-ers.

10 Numbers

We have seen that **un** and **una** mean 'a'. They are also used in the sense of 'one':

un home	a man <u>or</u> one man
una dona	a woman <u>or</u> one woman

The number 'two' also varies with gender:

dos homes	two men
dues dones	two women

Thereafter, no such distinction is made:

tres homes	three men
tres dones	three women

IMITATED PRONUNCIATION (10): doz 'o-mers; 'doo-erz 'don-ers; trayz 'o-mers; trayz 'don-ers.

11 'Some', 'a few'

The plural forms **uns** and **unes** are used in the sense of 'some':

unes dones	some women

Uns quants and **unes quantes** are used in the sense of 'a few'.

IMITATED PRONUNCIATION (11): oons; 'oon-ers; 'oon-erz 'don-ers; oons 'kwants; 'oon-es 'kwan-tes.

Vocabulary 3

l'amic (*m*)	friend (*m*)
l'amiga (*f*)	friend (*f*)
ample	wide
l'autobús (*m*)	bus
la botiga	shop
la caixa	bank
el despatx	office
estret	narrow; tight
el mes	month
negre	black; [of wine] red
el pis	flat; storey
el taxi	taxi
vermell	red

1 **un** (*masc.*), **una** (*fem.*)
2 **dos** (*masc.*), **dues** (*fem.*)
3 **tres**
4 **quatre**
5 **cinc**
6 **sis**
7 **set**
8 **vuit**
9 **nou**
10 **deu**

IMITATED PRONUNCIATION: er-'meek; er-'mee-ger; 'am-pler;
ah'oo-to-'booss; boo-'tee-ger; 'ka-sher; ders-'patch; ers-'trett;
mays; 'ne-grer; peace; taxi; ber-'mel-yer; oon; 'oon-er; doss;
'doo-ers; trays; 'kwat-trer; sing; sees; set; boo-'eet; 'no-oo;
'day-oo.

The **Eixample** (pronounced ay-'sham-pler) is an extensive area of
Barcelona built to a grid pattern in the second half of the
nineteenth century. The name means 'expansion'.

Exercise 3

Give the Catalan for:

1 Six Catalan towns.
2 Through the narrow streets of the Gothic Quarter.

3 Some rich women from the district.
4 The wide streets of the 'Eixample'.
5 The white churches.
6 The offices of the bank.
7 The shops in the square.
8 The rooms of the flat.
9 Those two flats.
10 Three red buses.
11 Four black and yellow taxis.
12 The teacher's children.

12 Negation

A statement may be put into the negative simply by inserting **no** before the verb:

La dona és catalana.
The woman is Catalan.
L'home no és català.
The man is not Catalan.

Gens may be used for emphasis with an adjective:

L'home no és gens llest.
The man is not at all clever.

Other negative concepts are expressed by using **no** together with a variety of elements, e.g.:

La dutxa no funciona mai.
The shower never works.
L'home no dóna res a la dona.
The man does not give anything to the woman.
L'home no menja cap peix.
The man does not eat (any) fish.

IMITATED PRONUNCIATION (12): no; ler 'don-er ays ker-ter-'lah-ner; 'lo-mer ays ker-ter-'lah; jens; 'lo-mer no ays jens lyest; ler 'doo-tcher no foonk-see-'own-er my; 'lo-mer no 'do-ner rez a ler 'don-er; 'lo-mer no 'men-jer cap pesh.

13 Accent marks

In the section on pronunciation we saw that accent marks are used to indicate where the stress in a word deviates from the usual practice. In some cases, however, an accent mark is used simply to distinguish one sense of a word from another. As we saw in the previous section, for example, an accent mark is used in **dóna** meaning 'gives' to distinguish it from **dona** meaning 'woman'. Other such pairs include the following:

sí	yes	**si**	if
és	is	**es**	itself, etc.
més	more	**mes**	month

IMITATED PRONUNCIATION (13): 'do-ner; see; ays; mays.

14 Talking to and about people

We have seen that the word **és** corresponds to 'is' in English. It may, however, be used when you are talking to a person as well as when you are talking about a person. This third person form of the verb is used when you are addressing somebody with whom you are not on informal terms. This practice, well known to speakers of Spanish, can be compared to such constructions in English as 'Your Highness is very kind'. In this case, because the third person is used for a variety of subjects, the pronouns, **vostè** in the singular and **vostès** in the plural, are more likely to be used:

És vostè anglès?
Are you English?

When talking to friends, relatives, children, etc. a Catalan will, on the other hand, use the second person of the verb:

Ets molt llest.
You are very clever.

When addressing somebody using a title (Mr, Mrs, etc.) no article is used:

Bon dia, senyor Puig.
Good day, Mr. Puig.

When talking about somebody to someone else, on the other hand, the definite article is used when a title is used:

El senyor Puig és molt llest.
Mr. Puig is very clever.

Members of a family may be referred to collectively as, for example, **els Puig** (cf. 'the Smiths').

An article is usually also used when referring to people by their fore-name:

La Maria i l'Antoni són llests.
Maria and Antoni are clever.

When referring to males whose name begins with a consonant the article used is **en**:

En Jaume no és llest.
Jaume is not clever.

IMITATED PRONUNCIATION (14): ays; boos-'tay; boos-'tays; ays boos-'tay ern-'gless; etts mol l'yest; bon'dee-er, sern-'yo pooch; erl sern-'yo pooch ays mol l'yest; erls pooch; ler mer-'ree-er ee lern-'tony son lyests; ern jah'oo-mer no ayz l'yest.

15 'To be'

The word **és** meaning 'is' belongs to the verb **ésser**. This is one of two verbs that Catalan has as equivalents of 'to be': **ésser** and **estar**.

The situations in which each verb is used corresponds in part to those that apply for the equivalent verbs in Spanish. The Catalan **ésser** is more widely used than is the Spanish 'ser', although the influence of Spanish is tending to extend the use of **estar**.

a) **Ésser** is used to refer to an inherent or permanent state of affairs. This includes nationality, profession and permanent location, e.g.:

Els plàtans són grocs.
Bananas are yellow.
L'home és català.
The man is Catalan.
És periodista.
He/she is a journalist.

L'església és a Girona.
The church is in Gerona.

IMITATED PRONUNCIATION (15a): ays; 'ays-er; erlz 'pla-terns son
grocks; 'lo-mer ays ker-ter-'lah; ays perry-od-'ist-er;
lerz-'glay-zee-er ayz er ji-'roh-ner.

b) **Estar** is used to refer to a more temporary state of affairs, such
as staying in a place for a specified period and state of health, e.g.:

La dona està a Girona fins demà.
The woman is in Gerona until tomorrow.
L'habitació està llesta.
The room is ready.
L'home està bé.
The man is well.

IMITATED PRONUNCIATION (15b): ler 'don-er erss-'tah er ji-'roh-ner
finz der-'mah; labby-tas-'yo erss-'tah l'yest-a; 'lo-mer erss-'tah bay.

c) Some adjectives may be used with either verb with a consequent
variation of meaning, e.g.:

L'home és llest.
The man is clever.
L'home està llest.
The man is ready.
L'home és content.
The man is happy. (*by nature*)
L'home està content.
The man is happy. (*for a particular reason*)

IMITATED PRONUNCIATION (15c): 'lo-mer ays l'yest; 'lo-mer erss-'tah
l'yest; 'lo-mer ays coon-'ten; 'lo-mer erss-'tah coon-'ten.

d) The present tense of each verb is as follows:

	(**ésser**)	(**estar**)
I am	**sóc**	**estic**
you are (*informal sing.*)	**ets**	**estàs**
he, etc. is	**és**	**està**
we are	**som**	**estem**
you are (*informal pl.*)	**sou**	**esteu**
they, etc. are	**són**	**estan**

IMITATED PRONUNCIATION (15d): 'ays-er; sock; etts; ays; som;
'so-oo; son; erss-'tah; ers-'tick; erss-'tahs; erss-'tah; erss-'tem;
erss-'tay-oo; erss-'tan.

16 Present tense of verbs ending in -ar

a) Many Catalan verbs end in **-ar** in the infinitive and take the
following forms in the present tense:

I work	**treballo**
you work (*informal sing.*)	**treballes**
he, etc. works	**treballa**
we work	**treballem**
you work (*informal pl.*)	**treballeu**
they, etc. work	**treballen**

Other verbs that follow this pattern include **parlar, passar** and
estudiar.

IMITATED PRONUNCIATION (16a): trer-'bal-yoo; trer-'bal-yers;
trer-'bal-yer; trer-berl-'yem; trer-berl-'yay-oo; trer-'berl-yern;
per-'la; perss-'a; erss-too-dee-'a.

b) Some verbs vary slightly. We have seen that **dóna** has an accent
mark to distinguish it from **dona** meaning 'woman'. So, too, **dónes**
has an accent mark to distinguish it from **dones** meaning 'women'.
As we saw with the plural, some amendments to the spelling are
required to retain the required sound before **e**, e.g.:

tancar (to close)	**jugar** (to play)
tanco	**jugo**
tanques	**jugues**
tanca	**juga**
tanquem	**juguem**
tanqueu	**jugueu**
tanquen	**juguen**

We saw with the plural form of **plaça** that a cedilla becomes
redundant before **e**; this also occurs with verbs like **començar** ('to
begin'):

començo	comencem
comences	comenceu
comença	comencen

Verbs in which the **-ar** follows immediately after a **j** change the **j** to **g** before **e**. Such verbs include **menjar** ('to eat'), **passejar** ('to go for a walk') and **viatjar** ('to travel').

IMITATED PRONUNCIATION (16b): 'don-er; 'don-er; 'don-erss; 'don-erss; tern-'ka; 'tan-koo; 'tan-kerss; 'tan-ker; tern-'kem; tern-'kay-oo; 'tan-kern; joo-'ga; 'joo-goo; 'joo-gerss; 'joo-ger; joo-'gaym; joo-'gay-oo; 'joo-gern; 'pla-ser; coom-ern-'sa; coom-'en-soo; coom-'en-serss; coom-'en-ser; coom-ern-'saym; coom-ern-'say-oo; coom-'en-sern; mern-'ja; pers-ser-'ja; bee-erd-'ja.

17 Use of the present tense

Catalan has a continuous tense like that of English to refer to an action that is taking place at the time of speaking:

Estic treballant.
I am working.

Often, however, Catalans use the simple present tense where we use the continuous tense.

Catalans also often use the present tense where we use a perfect tense or past tense to refer to a situation that began in the past but still applies at the time of speaking:

Treballo en aquesta caixa des de l'any 1991.
I have been working in this bank since 1991.
Fa tres anys que no treballo a la botiga.
It is three years since I worked in the shop.
or: I haven't worked in the shop for three years.

Note that the phrase **fa tres anys** can serve as an equivalent to 'three years ago'.

IMITATED PRONUNCIATION (17): er-'stick trer-ber-'lyan; trer-'bal-yoo ern er-'kest-er 'ca-sher dez der 'lanny meel 'no-oo cents noo-'rant-er oo; fa trayz annys ker no trer-'bal-yoo er ler boo-'tee-ger.

18 Prepositions 'a' and 'en'

The prepositions **a** and **en** can both equate to the English 'in' and it can be difficult to know when to use which, especially as the influence of Spanish compounds the confusion somewhat. **En** tends to be used before an indefinite article, **algun** or a demonstrative adjective such as **aquest**:

La dona treballa en una botiga.
The woman works in a shop.
No treballa en aquesta botiga.
She doesn't work in this shop.
La botiga és al passeig de Gràcia.
The shop is in the Passeig de Gràcia.

A is used with cities, countries, etc. as an equivalent to 'in' as well as to 'to':

Viatgen amb tren a França.
They are travelling by train to France.
Passen uns quants dies a Perpinyà.
They are spending a few days in Perpignan.

IMITATED PRONUNCIATION (18): ler 'do-ner trer-'bal-yer ern 'oon-er boo-'tee-ger; no trer-'bal-yer ern er-'kest-er boo-'tee-ger; ler boo-'tee-ger ayz erl per-'setch der 'gra-see-yer; bee-'adge-ern ern trayn er 'fran-ser; 'pa-sern oons kwantz 'dee-erz er per-pin-'ya.

19 'A ca'

A contraction of the word **casa** is used to give the phrase **a ca**, this meaning 'to/at the home/premises of':

En Jordi passa uns quants dies a ca l'Antoni.
Jordi is spending a few days at Antoni's (place).

When followed by **el**, **els** or **en**, **a ca** fuses with them:

a cal metge   to/at the doctor's
a can Pere   to/at Pere's (place)

IMITATED PRONUNCIATION (19): ern 'jor-di 'pa-ser oons kwantz 'dee-erz er ca lern-'toni; er cal 'metch-er; er cam 'pe-rer.

Vocabulary 4

	algun	some, any
	amb	with; [transport] by
	anglès	English
l'any (*m*)		year
	ara	now
	avui	today
	bé	well
	bell	beautiful
	com	how
	començar	to begin
	content	happy
	demà	tomorrow
	demà passat	the day after tomorrow
	des de	since, from
	donar	to give
la dutxa		shower
	en	in
	ésser	to be
	estar	to be
	estudiar	to study
	fa (tres anys)	(three years) ago
la família		family
	fer	to do, make
	fins (a)	as far as; until
	França	France
	funcionar	to work [function]
l'hospital (*m*)		hospital
	jugar	to play
	jugar a futbol	to play football
	llest	clever; ready
	menjar	to eat
el metge		doctor
la nit		night
	no	no; not
	o	or
el parc		park
	parlar (de)	to speak, to talk (about)
	passar	to pass, to spend [time]
el passeig		avenue
	passejar	to (go for a) walk

la pedra	stone
la pedrera	quarry
el peix	fish
el, la periodista	journalist
perquè	because; so that
el plàtan	banana; plane tree
sagrat	holy
el senyor	gentleman; Mr.
la senyora	lady; Mrs.
si	if
sí	yes
la sucursal	branch [of organisation]
tancar	to close
treballar	to work [employment]
el tren	train
viatjar	to travel

IMITATED PRONUNCIATION: erl-'goon; erm; ern-'gless; 'lan-yer; 'ah-rer; er-'vwee; bay; bell; kom; coom-ern-'sa; coon-'ten; der-'mah; der-'mah perss-'att; dez der; doo-'na; 'doo-cher; ern; 'ays-er; erss-'tah; erss-too-dee-'a; fah (trayz 'an-yers); fer-'meel-yer; fay; fins; 'fran-ser; foong-see-oon-'ar; oos-pi-'tal; joo-'ga; joo-'ga er foo-'bol; l'yest; mern-'ja; 'metch-er; neet; no; o; park; per-'la (der); perss-'a; per-'setch; per-ser-'ja; 'pe-drer; per-'dre-rer; pesh; perry-od-'ist-er; per-'ke; 'pla-tern; ser-'grat; sern-'yo; sern-'yor-er; see; see; soo-koor-'sal; tern-'ka; trer-berl-'ya; tren; bee-adge-'a.

Social phrases 2

Hola	Hello
Bon dia	Good day
Bona nit	Good night
Com està(s)?	How are you?
Molt bé	Very well
Adéu	Goodbye
Fins demà	Until tomorrow,
	See you tomorrow

IMITATED PRONUNCIATION: 'o-ler; bon 'dee-er; bonner neet; kom erss-'tah(s); mol bay; er-'day-oo; finz der-'mah.

Reading passage 2

Les obres més importants de Gaudí a la ciutat de Barcelona són el Parc Güell, la Casa Batlló, la Sagrada Família i la Pedrera o Casa Milà. La Casa Batlló i la Pedrera són al passeig de Gràcia. El passeig de Gràcia és el carrer més ample de l'Eixample.

Answer the following questions:

1 What distinguishes the Passeig de Gràcia?
2 What two famous buildings are to be found there?
3 Who designed them?

Exercise 4

Insert in each gap an appropriate form of **ésser** *or* **estar**

1 L'home _____ metge.
2 L'hospital on treballa _____ al carrer de Verdaguer.
3 Avui el metge no _____ a l'hospital.
4 El metge no _____ bé.
5 El fill de l'home _____ professor.
6 La dona del fill _____ anglesa.

Exercise 5

Give the Catalan for:

1 Mr. Puig works in a branch of the Caixa de Sabadell in the Passeig de Gràcia.
2 Jaume is a journalist.
3 Antoni is not a journalist.
4 He is a teacher.
5 Jaume and Antoni are happy because they are not working today.
6 They are playing football.
7 Maria is studying English.
8 She and a friend are going for a walk as far as the Plaça de Catalunya.
9 Maria is eating a banana.
10 Maria's friend is not eating anything.

CONVERSATION

La senyora Prat	Bon dia, senyor Puig. Com està? *Good morning, Mr. Puig. How are you?*
El senyor Puig	Molt bé, gràcies. *Very well, thank you.*
La senyora Prat	I la senyora Puig? *And Mrs. Puig?*
El senyor Puig	Bé. Passa uns quants dies a Girona amb una amiga. *Fine. She is spending a few days in Gerona with a friend.*
La senyora Prat	Girona és una ciutat bella. *Gerona is a beautiful city.*
El senyor Puig	Sí. *Yes.*
La senyora Prat	I com està en Jaume? *And how is Jaume?*
El senyor Puig	Molt bé. Ara és periodista. *Very well. He is a journalist now.*
La senyora Prat	Adéu. *Goodbye.*

Lesson 3

20 Present tense of verbs ending in -endre

Verbs that end in **-endre** in the infinitive take the following forms in the present tense:

I sell	**venc**
you sell (*informal sing.*)	**vens**
he, etc. sells	**ven**
we sell	**venem**
you sell (*informal pl.*)	**veneu**
they, etc. sell	**venen**

Verbs of more than two syllables, like **estendre** ('to stretch'), require a written accent in the third person singular: **estén**.

IMITATED PRONUNCIATION (20): beng; bens; ben; bern-'em; bern-'ay-oo; 'ben-ern; erss-'ten-drer; ers-'tayn.

21 Present tense of some irregular verbs

As in many languages, many common verbs do not share a pattern with numerous others and so have to be learnt individually. Such verbs include **beure** ('to drink'), **dir** ('to say'), **tenir** ('to have'), **viure** ('to live'), **anar** ('to go'), **fer** ('to do') and **voler** ('to want'):

beure	dir	tenir	viure
bec	dic	tinc	visc
beus	dius	tens	vius
beu	diu	té	viu
bevem	diem	tenim	vivim
beveu	dieu	teniu	viviu
beuen	diuen	tenen	viuen

As in the verbs of the **-endre** group and **ésser** and **estar**, the first person singular form of irregular verbs often ends in **c** as opposed to the usual **o**.

anar	fer	voler
vaig	faig	vull
vas	fas	vols
va	fa	vol
anem	fem	volem
aneu	feu	voleu
van	fan	volen

IMITATED PRONUNCIATION (21, infinitives only): 'bay-oo-rer; dee; ter-'nee; bee-'yoo-rer; er-'na; fay; boo-'lay.

22 Reflexive verbs

When a verb refers to an action done by the subject to himself, herself, etc. it is called a reflexive verb. In the first of the following sentences the simple verb **rentar** is used; in the second the verb is used reflexively:

La dona renta la camisa.
The woman is washing the shirt.
La dona es renta.
The woman is washing herself.

In the latter example we could simply say in English 'The woman is washing', but Catalan, like many languages, requires an object for the sentence to be considered complete. This is seen in the following example:

El carrer s'estén fins a la plaça.
The street stretches as far as the square.

Other verbs which have a reflexive form in Catalan while the English equivalent does not include **recordar-se de** and **queixar-se de**:

La dona es recorda de la casa.
The woman remembers the house.

When the infinitive is used the pronoun is often joined to the end as **-se** (**rentar-se**) or, following a vowel, as **'s** (**estendre's**). Otherwise it usually precedes the verb as **es** (**es renta**) or, before a vowel, as **s'** (**s'estén**).

These are the pronouns that accompany the third person forms, singular and plural, of the verb. For the first and second persons singular a similar pattern is followed using **m** and **t** respectively instead of **s**:

Em rento.
I am washing myself.
No vols rentar-te?
Do you not want to wash (yourself)?
No vols asseure't?
Do you not want to sit down?

The reflexive pronouns for the six persons are as follows when they precede a verb that begins with a consonant:

em	myself
et	yourself (*inform. sing.*)
es	himself, etc.
ens	ourselves
us	yourselves (*inform. pl.*)
es	themselves

Sometimes the reflexive form of a verb has a specific meaning. Thus the reflexive form of **dir** is the equivalent of 'to be called':

Diu que es diu Antoni.
He says that his name is Antoni.
Com es diu vostè?
What is your name?
Em dic John.
My name is John.

Similarly, **llevar** is 'to raise' while **llevar-se** is 'to get up', 'to get out of bed'.

The reflexive verb is also used to refer to a reciprocal action, an action which two or more people or things do to each other rather than to themselves:

Es troben a la plaça.
They meet (each other) in the square.

The reflexive verb is also used where it is not necessary to refer to the person or thing that carries out the action. In this case it often serves as an equivalent to the passive voice or the indeterminate subject 'they' in English:

Aquí es venen flors.
Flowers are sold here. *or* They sell flowers here.

IMITATED PRONUNCIATION (22): rern-'ta; ler 'don-er 'ren-ter ler ka-'mee-zer; ler 'don-er ez 'ren-ter; erl ker-'ray serss-'tayn finz er ler 'pla-ser; ler 'don-er erz rer-'corder der ler 'kahz-er; erm 'ren-too; no bolz rern-'tar-ter; no bolz er-'sayoo-rert; erm; ertt; erss; erns; oos; erss; dee'oo ker erss dee'oo ern-'tony; kom erss dee'oo boos-'tay; erm dick john; l'yer-'va; l'yer-'var-ser; erss 'tro-bern er ler 'pla-ser; er-'kee erz 'ben-ern floss.

23 Health

To tell somebody how you are, you might use the phrase **trobar-se bé**:

No em trobo bé.
I don't feel well.

To specify what is wrong with you, you can often use **tenir**:

Tinc mal de cap/de coll/d'estómac.
I have a sore head/throat/stomach.

IMITATED PRONUNCIATION (23): no erm 'troh-boo bay; ting mal der cap/der 'kol-yer/derss-'toh-merk.

24 Relative pronouns

The relative pronoun **que** is used to refer both to things and to people, whether they are subjects or objects of the clause. Thus it corresponds to 'that'/'which' and to 'who'/'whom' in English:

La dona que viu en aquesta casa és anglesa.
The woman who lives in this house is English.
La casa que l'home ven és vella.
The house that the man is selling is old.

Following a preposition, **què** is used in respect of things and **qui** is used in respect of people:

Els plàtans sota què passeja són alts.
The plane trees under which he is walking are tall.
La dona amb qui passeja és anglesa.
The woman with whom he is walking is English.

Alternatively, the compound forms **el qual, la qual, els quals** and **les quals** may be used:

La dona, la qual viu en aquesta casa, és anglesa.
Els plàtans sota els quals passeja són alts.

Being variable, this compound form may allow confusion to be avoided. Thus in the following example the use of a masculine pronoun makes it clear that it is the son and not the woman who works in the bank:

El fill de la dona, el qual treballa a la caixa, viu a Sitges.
The son of the woman, who works in the bank, lives in Sitges.

Used with an article, **qui** means 'he who', 'those who', etc.:

Els qui viuen en aquesta casa són molt rics.
The people who live in this house are very rich.

In the sense of 'that which', 'what' is translated by **el que**:

No diu el que vol fer.
He is not saying what he wants to do.

IMITATED PRONUNCIATION (24): ler 'don-er ker bee'oo ern er-'kest-er 'kahz-er ayz ern-'glez-er; ler 'kahz-er ker 'lo-mer ben ays bella; erls 'pla-terns 'soh-ter ke per-'say-jer son alts; ler 'don-er erm key per-'say-jer ayz ern-'glez-er; erl kwal; ler kwal; erls kwals; lers kwals; ler 'don-er, ler kwal bee'oo ern er-'kest-er 'kah-zer, ayz ern-'glez-er; erls 'pla-terns 'soh-ter erls kwals per-'say-jer son alts; erl 'fil-yer der ler 'don-er, erl kwal trer-'bal-yer er ler 'ka-sher, bee'oo er 'sit-jers; erls key bee-'oo-ern ern er-'kest-er 'kahz-er son mol reeks; no dee'oo erl ker bol fay.

Vocabulary 5

l'aigua (*f*)	water
alt	tall, high

anar	to go
aquí	here
asseure's	to sit down
beure	to drink
la camisa	shirt
el cap	head
cap a	towards; [time] at about
el coll	neck; throat
el diari	newspaper
dir	to say, tell
dir-se	to be called
estendre('s)	to stretch
l'estómac (*m*)	stomach
la filla	daughter
la flor	flower
la font	fountain, spring
llevar	to raise; to remove
llevar-se	to get up
Londres	London
el mar	sea
l'ocell (*m*)	bird
què?	what?
quedar-se	to stay, remain
queixar-se (de)	to complain (about)
recordar-se (de)	to remember
rentar(-se)	to wash
sempre	always
el símbol	symbol
sota	under
tenir	to have
trobar	to meet; to find
vendre	to sell
viure	to live
voler	to want

IMITATED PRONUNCIATION: 'ay-gwer; al; er-'na; er-'key;
er-'say-ooers; 'bay-oo-rer; ka-'mee-zer; cap; cap er; 'kol-yer;
dee-'ar-ee; dee; 'dee-ser; erss-'ten-drer(s); erss-'tomak; 'feel-yer; flo;
fon; l'yer-'va; l'yer-'var-ser; 'lon-drerss; mar; oo-'sel-yer; key;
ker-'dar-ser; ker-'shar-ser; rer-kor-'dar-ser; rern-'ta;
'sem-prer; 'sim-bool; 'so-ter; tern-'ee; troo-'ba; 'ben-drer;
bee-'yoo-rer; boo-'lay.

Reading passage 3

La Rambla s'estén de la plaça de Catalunya fins al mar. Aquí, sota els plàtans, es venen diaris, flors i ocells. La Font de Canaletes és al capdamunt de la Rambla, prop de la plaça de Catalunya. La font és un dels símbols de la ciutat. Es diu que el qui beu aigua de la Font de Canaletes es queda per sempre més a viure a Barcelona.

Answer the following questions:

1 Where does one arrive if one walks all the way down the Rambla from the Plaça de Catalunya?
2 What can you buy in the Rambla?
3 Where is the Font de Canaletes?
4 What is supposed to happen if one drinks from the fountain?

Exercise 6

Reply to the following questions as indicated by the prompt word in brackets.

Example: Com es diu vostè? (Anne) Em dic Anne.

1 Què vols fer? (play football)
2 Què vols menjar? (fish)
3 Què vol menjar la dona? (nothing)
4 Com estàs? (headache)
5 Vius a Londres? (Manchester)
6 On treballes? (a shop)

Exercise 7

Give the Catalan for:

1 Mr. Puig lives in a flat in the Carrer Pau Claris.
2 The flat has five rooms.
3 Mr. Puig has three sons and a daughter.
4 The daughter is called Maria.
5 She is studying English at the University of Barcelona.
6 What is the teacher called?
7 He is called Brian Mott.
8 He is from London but he has lived in Barcelona since 1972.

25 Past tense

Having learnt the verb **anar**, it is a short step to being able to refer to actions that took place in the past. One simply has to learn a variation on the verb **anar** and then use that together with the relevant infinitive:

El nen va menjar el plàtan.
The boy ate the banana.
Vam vendre la casa.
We sold the house.

In this tense pronouns may either stand before the verb or be appended to the infinitive:

Em vaig llevar./Vaig llevar-me.
I got up.

The forms of the auxiliary verb are as follows:

vaig
vas
va
vam
vau
van

This tense is used to refer to a single action completed in the past.

IMITATED PRONUNCIATION (25): erl nen ba mern-'ja erl 'pla-tern;
bam 'ben-drer ler 'kah-zer; erm batch l'yer-'va;
batch l'yer-'bar-mer; batch; bas; ba; bam; bah'oo; ban.

26 Constructions with 'tenir'

Catalans use the verb **tenir** in a number of situations where we use 'to be'. They 'have hunger', for example:

L'home té molta gana.	The man is very hungry.
Té set també.	He is also thirsty.
Tinc ganes de fer això.	I want to do this.
Tens calor?	Are you hot?
Tinc pressa.	I am in a hurry.

Tenir is also used to express age:

Quants anys té la nena?	How old is the girl?
Té sis anys.	She is six years old.

IMITATED PRONUNCIATION (26): 'lo-mer tay molta 'gah-ner; tay set term-'bay; ting 'gah-ners der fay ersh-'o; tens ker-'lor; ting 'press-er; tern-'ee; kwants annys tay ler 'nen-er; tay sees annys.

27 Time of day

Quina hora és?	What time is it?
Són les tres.	It is three o'clock.

When referring to one o'clock the singular is used:

És la una.	It is one o'clock.

When referring to two o'clock the number, like the article, has to be in the feminine to agree with **hora**:

Són les dues.	It is two o'clock.

Even when referring to half past the hour, Catalan expresses the time in terms of quarters passed on the way to the next hour:

És un quart de quatre.	It is a quarter past three.
Són dos quarts de quatre.	It is half past three.
Són tres quarts de quatre.	It is a quarter to four.

Quarts de is sometimes used as an approximate equivalent to 'half past':

Són quarts de quatre.	It is (about) half past three.

For other times **i** equates to 'past' and **menys** equates to 'to':

Són les quatre i deu.	It is ten past four.
Són les cinc menys cinc.	It is five minutes to five.

When asking when something happens the phrase **a quina hora?** is used:

A quina hora es tanca la botiga?
When does the shop shut?

The reply also uses **a**, this replacing **és/són**:

Es tanca a les vuit.
It shuts at eight o'clock.

Del matí, de la tarda, etc. may be used to specify the part of the day:

L'avió arriba a les quatre de la tarda.
The plane arrives at four in the afternoon.

To avoid being too precise, one may use **cap a**:

L'avió arriba cap a les quatre.
The plane arrives at about four o'clock.
Esmorzo cap a les vuit.
I have breakfast at about eight o'clock.

IMITATED PRONUNCIATION (27): keen or ays; son lers trays; ayz ler 'oon-er; son lers 'doo-ers; ayz oon kwar der 'kwat-rer; son trays kwarts der 'kwat-rer; son kwarts der 'kwat-rer; ee; 'men-yis; son lers 'kwat-rer ee 'day-oo; son lers sing 'men-yis sing; er 'kee-ner or-er erss 'tan-ker ler boo-'teeger; erss 'tan-ker er lers boo-eet; derl mer-'tee; der ler 'tar-der; ler-ve-'o er-'ree-ber er lers 'kwat-rer der ler 'tar-der, ler-ve-'o er-'ree-ber cap er lers 'kwat-rer; er-'moor-zoo cap er lers boo'eet.

Vocabulary 6

això	this, that
arribar	to arrive
avall	down
l'avió (*m*)	plane
la calor	heat
castellà	Castilian, Spanish
la cervesa	beer
el cinema	cinema
comprar	to buy
la copa	glass
la cosa	thing
escocès	Scottish
esmorzar	to have breakfast
l'estudiant (*m*)	student
fer la copa	to have a drink
la festa	party; festival
la gana	hunger

l'hora (f)	hour
el matí	morning
menys	less, minus
el nen	young boy
la nena	young girl
el noi	lad, guy
obert	open
la pel.lícula	film
per què?	why?
la porta	door
la pressa	hurry
de pressa	quickly
quant?	how much?
quants?	how many?
qui?	who?
quin?	which?
la set	thirst
també	also, as well
la tarda	afternoon

11 onze
12 dotze
13 tretze
14 catorze
15 quinze
16 setze
17 disset
18 divuit
19 dinou
20 vint

IMITATED PRONUNCIATION: er-'shor; er-ri-'ba; er-'val-yer; ler-vi-'yo; ler ker-'lo; ker-ster-'lya; ser-'vay-zer; ci-'ne-mer; coom-'pra; ler 'co-per; ler 'co-zer; ers-coo-'ses; erz-moor-'za; lers-too-dee-'yan; fay ler 'co-per; ler 'fes-ter; ler 'ga-ner; 'lo-rer; erl mer-'tee; 'men-yis; erl nen; ler 'ne-ner; erl noy; oo-'ber; ler perl-'li-coo-ler; per-'ke; ler 'por-ter; ler 'pre-ser; der 'pre-ser; kwan; kwants; kee; keen; ler set; term-'bay; ler 'tar-der.

'on-zer; 'dod-zer; 'tred-zer; ker-'tor-zer; 'kin-zer; 'sed-zer; di-'set; di-'bweet; di-'no-oo; bin.

Exercise 8

Put the following sentences into the past tense.

1 L'home renta el cotxe.
2 En Joan beu el vi.
3 Vas al mar?
4 Juguen a futbol.
5 Venem el pis.
6 El metge tanca la porta.

Exercise 9

Reply to the following questions as indicated by the time in brackets.

Example: Quina hora és? (7.00) Són les set.

1 Quina hora és? (5.20)
2 Quina hora és? (4.50)
3 Quina hora és? (1.15)
4 A quina hora es tanca la caixa? (1.30)
5 A quina hora comença la festa? (about 8.00)
6 A quina hora arriba el tren? (10.10 a.m.)

Exercise 10

Give the Catalan for:

1 Pere and Maria are going to the cinema.
2 At what time does the film start?
3 It starts at eight o'clock.
4 They meet in the square at a quarter to eight.
5 At what time does the bank close?
6 It is open from nine o'clock until two o'clock.
7 How old is Mark?
8 He is twenty years old.
9 He got up at half past nine.
10 Who washed the shirt?
11 The young girl does not want to wash herself.
12 The man who sold the flat lives in Sitges.

CONVERSATION

Don't forget that you should read these dialogues aloud; if you have the audio cassettes, listen carefully and copy what you hear. Note all the new vocabulary and constructions, together with the use of idioms. Incidentally, there'll be no imitated pronunciation from Lesson 4.

La Maria	Què vols fer? Per què no anem la Rambla avall? *What do you want to do? Why don't we go down the Rambla?*
En Pere	Vaig a fer la copa amb un noi escocès. Vols fer això? *I'm going to have a drink with a Scottish guy. Do you want to do that?*
La Maria	Sí. *Yes.*
En Pere	Ens trobem al capdamunt de la Rambla, a la Font de Canaletes. *We are meeting at the top of the Rambla, at the Font de Canaletes.*
La Maria	A quina hora? *At what time?*
En Pere	A dos quarts de cinc. *At half past four.*
La Maria	Com es diu? *What is his name?*
En Pere	Mark. *Mark.*
La Maria	Què fa aquí? És estudiant? *What is he doing here? Is he a student?*
En Pere	Sí. Estudia castellà. *Yes. He is studying Spanish.*
La Maria	Vols beure alguna cosa ara? *Do you want anything to drink now?*
En Pere	Sí. Tinc molta set. *Yes. I'm very thirsty.*

La Maria   Què vols beure? Tenim aigua mineral Font
Vella i cervesa.
*What do you want to drink? We've got Font Vella
mineral water and beer.*

En Pere   Cervesa.
Beer.

Lesson 4

28 Present tense of verbs ending in -ir

Verbs that end in **-ir** in the infinitive generally have the following endings in the present tense:

I open	**obro**
you open (*informal sing.*)	**obres**
he, etc. opens	**obre**
we open	**obrim**
you open (*informal plural*)	**obriu**
they open	**obren**

A great many of the **-ir** verbs, however, insert the element **-eix-** before the ending in the singular forms and in the third person plural of the present tense:

I read	**llegeixo**
you read (*informal sing.*)	**llegeixes**
he, etc. reads	**llegeix**
we read	**llegim**
you read (*informal plural*)	**llegiu**
they read	**llegeixen**

29 Present tense of some irregular verbs

escriure	**veure**	**creure**
(to write)	(to see)	(to believe)
escric	**veig**	**crec**
escrius	**veus**	**creus**
escriu	**veu**	**creu**
escrivim	**veiem**	**creiem**
escriviu	**veieu**	**creieu**
escriuen	**veuen**	**creuen**

30 Object pronouns (first and second persons)

In Lesson 3 reflexive verbs were introduced. There, examples of
the first and second person reflexive pronouns were seen:

Em rento.
No vols rentar-te?

These pronouns are also used when the subject and the object of
the sentence relate to different people:

L'home em va donar un plàtan.
The man gave me a banana.

In the first and second persons no distinction need be made
between direct and indirect objects:

L'home em va veure a Vic.
The man saw me in Vic.
L'home em va escriure una carta.
The man wrote me a letter.

As we saw, the form of the pronoun depends on whether it stands
before the verb or is suffixed to it and on whether it stands next to
a consonant or a vowel, e.g.:

L'home no vol donar-me el diari.
The man does not want to give me the newspaper.
La dona no vol vendre'm el pis.
The woman does not want to sell me the flat.

The following table sets out the various forms of the first and
second person object pronouns:

	before consonant	before vowel	after consonant	after vowel
1st singular	**em**	**m'**	**-me**	**'m**
2nd singular	**et**	**t'**	**-te**	**'t**
1st plural	**ens**	**ens**	**-nos**	**'ns**
2nd plural	**us**	**us**	**-vos**	**-us**

The apostrophe is used where the vowel of the pronoun has been
lost.

52

Vocabulary 7

la carta	letter
creure	to believe, think
darrera (de)	behind
darrere (de)	behind
davant (de)	in front (of)
escriure	to write
llegir	to read
el museu	museum
obrir	to open
veure	to see

Exercise 11

Give the Catalan for:

1 The man is reading a newspaper.
2 He does not want to open the door.
3 He saw me with Maria in front of the cathedral.
4 Maria wrote me a letter in English.
5 I read (past tense) the letter on the bus.
6 She told me what she wants to do the day after tomorrow.
7 She wants to go to the museum in the park.
8 At what time does the museum open?
9 I think that it opens at ten o'clock.
10 I don't want to go to the museum.

31 Expressing opinions

When saying that he likes something a Catalan, like other Spaniards, often says that that thing pleases him. Thus he is the object, not the subject, of the sentence:

M'agrada aquest cotxe.
I like this car.
A en Pere li agrada jugar a futbol.
Pere likes playing football.

It follows, too, that the verb takes the plural form if it is more than one thing that pleases him:

M'agraden els cotxes.
I like cars.
No m'agraden els plàtans.
I don't like bananas.

To emphasise one's liking of something, one can add **molt**:

M'agrada molt el cotxe.
I like the car very much.

To emphasise one's dislike of something, one can add **gens** or **ni mica**:

No m'agrada gens el cotxe.
I don't like the car at all.

Strong dislike can also be expressed by the phrase **fer fàstic**:

El peix em fa fàstic.
I detest fish.

When comparing one thing with another one can use either of the following forms:

M'agrada més el vi negre.
M'estimo més el vi negre. ⎫ I prefer red wine.
Prefereixo el vi negre. ⎭

Note that while it is the thing preferred that is the grammatical subject of **M'agrada més el vi negre** it is, as in English, the person who prefers who is the subject of **M'estimo més el vi negre**.

To express an opinion about something you may need the verb **semblar** or the verb **pensar**:

Què et sembla el vi?
What do you think of the wine?
Em sembla que el vi blanc és millor que el vi negre.
I think that the white wine is better than the red wine.
Penso que aquest vi és massa car.
I think that this wine is too expensive.

32 Omission of nouns

When it is clear what we are talking about we may replace a noun by the word 'one' in English. In Catalan one can simply omit the noun without replacing it with anything:

M'agrada la camisa blanca però prefereixo la groga.
I like the white shirt but I prefer the yellow one.
Prefereixes aquesta?
Do you prefer this one?

Similarly, nouns may be omitted in situations like the following:

Veig el cotxe d'en Pere i el d'en Jordi.
I see Pere's car and Jordi's.

33 Numbers

We have seen that 'twenty' is **vint**. Units are added to **vint** using the conjunction **i**, the word for 'and', between hyphens, e.g.:

vint-i-quatre   twenty-four

From the thirties onwards, however, **i** is not used, e.g.:

trenta-quatre   thirty-four

From 'two hundred' onwards the word for 'hundred', **cent**, is joined to its multiplier by a hyphen. It takes a feminine form if appropriate. This applies, for example, when it is used in the context of Spanish currency as **pesseta** is feminine:

El vi és quatre-centes pessetes.
The wine is four hundred pesetas.

The word for 'thousand', **mil**, is, on the other hand, invariable and it is not accompanied by a hyphen:

Sitges té quinze mil habitants.
Sitges has fifteen thousand inhabitants.

The word for 'million', **milió**, is a noun and consequently is accompanied by **de** when it is used to count other nouns:

Barcelona té dos milions d'habitants.
Barcelona has two million inhabitants.

As an example of the combination of thousands, hundreds, tens and units, the year 1995 would be expressed as follows:

Mil nou-cents noranta-cinc.

Vocabulary 8

agradar	to please
allà	there
altre	other
assemblar-se a	to resemble
ballar	to dance
el **cap de setmana**	weekend
car	dear, expensive
el **costat**	side
el **cotó**	cotton
el **dependent** (*m*) la **dependenta** (*f*)	employee; shop assistant
el **diccionari**	dictionary
l'**entrada** (*f*)	entrance; ticket [for admission]
entrar (**a**/**en**)	to enter (into)
l'**est**	east
estimar	to like, love
estimar-se més	to prefer
el **fàstic**	loathing, revulsion
formar	to form
la **frontera**	border
l'**habitant** (*m*/*f*)	inhabitant
massa	too (many)
mediterrani	Mediterranean
una **mica**	a little
la **muntanya**	mountain
muntanyós	mountainous
el **nord**	north
pensar	to think
la **pesseta**	peseta
els **Pirineus**	Pyrenees
la **planura**	plain
la **platja**	beach
la **postal**	postcard
preferir (★)	to prefer
la **província**	province

la ratlla	stripe
sec	dry
semblar	to seem
la setmana	week
el sud	south
el tennis	tennis
el triangle	triangle

(*) The verb **preferir** inserts **-eix-**.

30 **trenta**
40 **quaranta**
50 **cinquanta**
60 **seixanta**
70 **setanta**
80 **vuitanta**
90 **noranta**
100 **cent**
1,000 **mil**
1,000,000 **un milió**

Social phrases 3

Si us plau   Please

Reading passage 4

Catalunya s'assembla a un triangle. Un costat, el del nord, és els Pirineus. Allà fa frontera amb França. Un altre costat és la costa mediterrània. Les muntanyes i el mar es troben formant la Costa Brava. La costa al sud de Barcelona es diu la Costa Daurada. Les províncies de l'est són muntanyoses. Les planures de l'interior, de la província de Lleida, són més seques.

Answer the following questions:

1 On which side of Catalonia lie the Pyrenees?
2 What meet to form the Costa Brava?
3 What characterises the climate of the plains of the province of Lleida?

Exercise 12

*Express your opinion of the following in accordance with the prompts
(√ = like, √√ = like a lot, X = don't like, XX = don't like at all).*

1 Red wine (√)
2 Beer (X)
3 To travel (√√)
4 Bananas (XX)
5 This flat (√√)
6 To play tennis (X)

Exercise 13

*Reply to the following questions as indicated by the figure in brackets.
These figures represent Spanish currency, referred to in Catalan as
'pessetes'.*

1 Quant és el diccionari? (3600)
2 Quant és l'entrada al museu? (350)
3 Quant és aquesta postal? (45)
4 Quant és la camisa blanca? (2500)
5 Quant és la groga? (2650)
6 Quant són aquestes flors? (480)

Exercise 14

Give the Catalan for:

1 What do you think of the red wine?
2 I don't like red wine at all.
3 I prefer white wine.
4 Do you like drinking beer?
5 Yes, I like beer a lot.
6 I drink a lot of beer.
7 Do you like living in Barcelona?
8 Yes, but I like to spend weekends in Sitges.
9 I have had a flat in Sitges since 1990.
10 I have a friend (female) there who is a shop assistant.
11 She is twenty-six years old.
12 We like to spend a few hours on the beach.

CONVERSATION

En Pere Vull comprar una camisa. Què et sembla aquesta blava?
I want to buy a shirt. What do you think of this blue one?

La Maria No m'agrada. Prefereixo aquesta blanca de ratlles.
I don't like it. I prefer this white one with stripes.

En Pere És massa estreta. T'agrada aquesta groga?
It's too tight. Do you like this yellow one?

La Maria Sí. És de cotó, oi?
Yes. It's cotton, isn't it?

En Pere Crec que sí.
I think so.

La Maria Quant és?
How much is it?

En Pere Quatre mil vuit-centes pessetes.
Four thousand eight hundred pesetas.

La Maria És una mica cara.
It's a bit expensive.

En Pere Sí, però m'agrada molt.
Yes, but I like it a lot.

(a la dependenta) Aquesta camisa, si us plau.
(to the shop assistant) This shirt, please.

La dependenta Alguna cosa més?
Anything else?

En Pere No, res més.
No, nothing else.

Lesson 5

34 Object pronouns (third person)

In Lesson 4 we saw that in the case of the first and second persons the object pronouns are the same as the reflexive pronouns. This is not the case with the third person:

El gos es va rentar.
The dog washed itself.
La dona el va rentar.
The woman washed it.

It will be seen that in this case the pronoun is the same as the definite article, the word for 'the'. When standing in front of a verb the form of the direct object pronoun follows the same principles as the form of the definite article:

Vaig comprar les camises.
I bought the shirts.
Les vaig comprar.
I bought them.

Vaig veure les dones.
I saw the women.
Les vaig veure.
I saw them.

La Maria escriu la carta.
Maria is writing the letter.
La Maria l'escriu.
Maria is writing it.

It will be seen, too, that these pronouns refer to both things and people, as 'them' does in English. Thus:

La vaig veure a la plaça.
I saw it/her in the square.

In English the pronoun 'him' has a different function in the sentences "I hit him" and "I sold him the flat".

In the second example it is 'the flat' that is being sold, not 'him'. In this case 'him' is an indirect object, it indicating not what is being sold but to whom the thing is being sold. In Catalan the indirect object pronouns are **li** in the singular and **els** in the plural when standing before the verb. No distinction is made for gender:

Li vaig vendre el pis.
I sold him/her the flat.

As with the first and second person pronouns, those of the third person take different forms when they are suffixed to an infinitive:

Vull vendre'l.
I want to sell it.
Vull donar-los el diari.
I want to give them the newspaper.

The following table sets out the forms of the third person object pronouns. In the case of the direct object pronouns two forms are given, these being masculine and feminine. In the case of the indirect object pronouns no distinction is made for gender.

	before consonant	before vowel	after consonant	after vowel
direct sing.	**el, la**	**l'** (*)	**-lo, -la**	**'l, -la**
direct plur.	**els, les**	**els, les**	**-los, -les**	**'ls, -les**
indirect sing.	**li**	**li**	**-li**	**-li**
indirect plur.	**els**	**els**	**-los**	**'ls**

(*) As with the definite article, the feminine pronoun is **la** before unstressed **i** (**hi**) or **u** (**hu**).

Where the pronoun does not represent a specific noun a neuter pronoun, **ho**, is used:

No vull fer-ho.
I do not want to do it.

This pronoun may be required to provide an object where none is provided in English:

No ho sap.
He doesn't know.

Its form does not change.

35 The pronouns 'en' and 'hi'

These two pronouns will present little difficulty to those acquainted with the French equivalents 'en' and 'y'. They represent a combination of a preposition and a pronoun.

● **En** basically stands for the preposition **de** plus a pronoun:

No em recordo de la dona.
I don't remember the woman.
No me'n recordo.
I don't remember her.

Parlen molt dels fills.
They talk a lot about the children.
En parlen molt.
They talk a lot about them.

L'home va tornar de Sitges.
The man came back from Sitges.
L'home en va tornar.
The man came back from there.

This pronoun, too, may be required to represent an object that is not represented in English:

Tinc cinc fills.
I have five children.
En tinc cinc.
I have five (of them).

● **Hi** may stand for other prepositions plus a pronoun. It may correspond to the English adverb 'there':

Vaig anar a la ciutat.
I went to the town.
Hi vaig anar.
I went there.

Hi does not change but **en** does, it changing in the same way as do **em**, **et** and **es**:

No vull anar-hi.
I don't want to go there.
No vull parlar-ne.
I don't want to talk about it.

The phrase **hi ha** means 'there is' or 'there are':

Hi ha tres hotels a la plaça.
There are three hotels in the square.

36 Perfect tense

In English we can say 'He has closed the door'. Similarly, Catalans can say **Ha tancat la porta**. This is the perfect tense. To construct it we need the equivalent of the verb 'to have' and a past participle.

Catalan has two verbs that equate to 'to have'. We have already seen **tenir**, which refers to possession:

Tinc un cotxe.
I have a car.

The perfect tense, however, is formed with another verb, **haver**, a verb that we have just seen in the phrase **hi ha**. Its forms in the present tense are as follows:

he	**hem**
has	**heu**
ha	**han**

The form of the past participle depends on the class of verb. In the case of **-ar** verbs and **-ir** verbs it usually ends in **-at** and **-it** respectively. Thus, quite simply, the **r** of the infinitive is replaced by **t**:

He tancat la porta.
I have closed the door.
He llegit el diari.
I have read the newspaper.

In the case of verbs ending in **-endre** the past participle usually ends in **-ès**:

No he entès el que va dir.
I haven't understood what he said.

Other past participles end in **-ut**:

He perdut una targeta de crèdit.
I have lost a credit card.

Some verbs have an irregular past participle:

beure – begut
creure – cregut
escriure – escrit
ésser – estat
fer – fet
haver – hagut
obrir – obert
tenir – tingut
vendre – venut
veure – vist
viure – viscut
voler – volgut

When an object pronoun is used, the past participle agrees with it:

He tancat la porta.
I have closed the door.
L'he tancada.
I have closed it.

As in English, the past participle may be used to refer to a state rather than an action. It then agrees where appropriate with the noun to which it is referring, like any other adjective:

L'obra és inacabada.
The work is unfinished.

The past participle may occasionally also serve as a noun:

Vaig trobar un conegut.
I met an acquaintance.

Some nouns are derived from the feminine form of the past participle. Over a door you might see **entrada** or **sortida**. In a railway station you will see **sortides** in the sense of 'departures'. Before departing, you might buy **un bitllet d'anada i tornada**, a return ticket. From the train you might enjoy the **vista**.

When referring to something done in the immediate past Catalan uses the phrase **acabar de** followed by the infinitive:

Acabo de fer-ho.
I have just done it.

37 Obligation

The verb **haver** is also used, together with the preposition **de**, to express obligation, to say that one has to do something:

En Pere ha de treballar.
Pere has to work.

In this context, it is usual to use a variant of the first person singular form, **haig** rather than **he**:

Haig de fer-ho avui.
I have to do it today.

38 Present tense of some irregular verbs

poder	**saber**	**venir**
(to be able)	(to know)	(to come)
puc	sé	vinc
pots	saps	véns
pot	sap	ve
podem	sabem	venim
podeu	sabeu	veniu
poden	saben	vénen

conèixer	**sortir**
(to know)	(to leave)
conec	surto
coneixes	surts
coneix	surt
coneixem	sortim
coneixeu	sortiu
coneixen	surten

Note that two of the forms of **venir** have an accent mark, this serving to distinguish them from the equivalent forms of **vendre**.

Vocabulary 9

acabar	to finish, complete
acabar de	to have just
l'accident (*m*)	accident

el bitllet	ticket [to travel]
el bitllet d'anada i tornada	return ticket
el conegut (*m*)	acquaintance
la coneguda {*f*}	
conèixer	(to get) to know [person, place]
entendre	to understand
la farmàcia	pharmacy, chemist's
el gos	dog
l'hotel (*m*)	hotel
perdre	to lose
poder	to be able (to)
saber	to know [fact]
la sortida	exit; departure
sortir	to leave, go out, depart
la targeta de crèdit	credit card
tornar	to return, go/come back
tornar a	to . . . again
venir	to come
la vista	view

Exercise 15

Rewrite the following sentences substituting the appropriate equivalent of 'it', 'them', 'to her', etc. for the words in brackets.

Example: La dona llegeix (el diari). La dona el llegeix.

1 La nena no vol menjar (els plàtans).
2 He perdut (els bitllets).
3 No puc obrir (la porta).
4 No vull parlar (de l'accident).
5 Vull donar les flors (a la dona).
6 Vaig escriure (a l'Antoni).

Exercise 16

Give the Catalan for:

1 I have just bought a shirt.
2 I also like this one but I don't want to buy it.
3 How many shirts do you have?
4 I have many.
5 Do you know if there is a chemist's near here?

6 Have you seen Maria?
7 Yes, I saw her on the beach.
8 Have you given her the newspaper?
9 No, I want to read it again.
10 I know that he wants to do it tomorrow.
11 But I cannot go there tomorrow.
12 I have to work at the hotel until seven o'clock.

39 Making requests

To ask or tell somebody to do something, the imperative form of the verb may be used:

Dóna el diari a la Maria.   Give the newspaper to Maria.

We have seen that pronouns are often appended to the end of infinitives. They are also appended to imperatives:

Dóna-li el diari.   Give her the newspaper.

The above examples are using the second person, the informal form of address. For **-ar** verbs this ends in **a** when addressing one person and **eu** when addressing more than one person. For **-ir** verbs there is no ending in the singular, the stem alone being used, together with the element **-eix-** where appropriate, and in the plural the verb ends in **-iu**:

Torneu demà.   Come back tomorrow.
Llegeix aquesta carta.   Read this letter.

In the third person, when talking to people whom one would address as **vostè**, the verb ends in **i** when addressing one person and in **in** when addressing more than one:

Perdoni.   Excuse me.
Posi'm dos quilos de tomàquets. Give me two kilos of tomatoes.

The imperative forms for some of the irregular verbs seen so far are as follows:

	anar	dir	fer
sing. inform.	vés	digues	fes
plur. inform.	aneu	digueu	feu
sing. formal	vagi	digui	faci
plur. formal	vagin	diguin	facin

Catalans often say **digui** when receiving a telephone call.

In English a request can be made more polite by using such phrases as 'Would you please close . . .?', 'Would you mind closing . . .?'. In Catalan a request to close a door might similarly be expressed as follows:

Pots tancar la porta?
Et fa res tancar la porta?

40 Adverbs

Adverbs, words used to qualify a verb or an adjective, are often formed by adding **-ment** to the feminine form of the adjective:

El cotxe és ràpid.	The car is fast.
El cotxe va ràpidament.	The car goes fast.

As the above example shows, any accent mark in the adjective is retained in the adverb despite any change in stress.

In Catalan a phrase will often be used to fulfil the same function. Thus, for example, the phrase **de pressa** has a similar meaning to **ràpidament**:

Haig de fer-ho de pressa.
I have to do it quickly.

The comparative and superlative forms of adverbs are constructed in the same way as those of adjectives:

El cotxe d'en Jaume va més ràpidament.
Jaume's car goes faster.

41 Gerund

Lesson 2 referred briefly to a continuous tense. This is formed from **estar** and the gerund. Like equivalents in English such as 'I am reading', it emphasises that the action is in progress at the time concerned. The gerund ends in **-ant**, **-ent**, or **-int** depending on the class of verb:

Està canviant uns xecs de viatge.
He/she is changing some travellers' cheques.
Estic llegint una guia.
I am reading a guidebook.

Note that the infinitive, not the gerund, is used after a preposition:

Després d'aparcar el cotxe em va donar la clau.
After parking the car he/she gave me the key.

42 Days of the week

The days of the week are as follows:

Monday	**dilluns**	Friday	**divendres**
Tuesday	**dimarts**	Saturday	**dissabte**
Wednesday	**dimecres**	Sunday	**diumenge**
Thursday	**dijous**		

Where in English we use 'on' with a day of the week, Catalans use the definite article or nothing:

Vull fer-ho (el) dijous.
I want to do it on Thursday.

When referring to a regular occurrence the plural article is used and those days of the week that do not end in an **s**, **dissabte** and **diumenge**, acquire a plural **s**:

Treballo els dissabtes.
I work on Saturdays.

Vocabulary 10

aparcar	to park
l'ascensor (*m*)	lift
canviar	to change
el cau	den
la clau	key
el començament	beginning
construir (⋆)	to build
després (**de**)	after
dirigir (⋆)	to direct

(⋆) The verbs **construir** and **dirigir** insert **-eix-**.

l'edifici (*m*)	building
encara	still
ensenyar	to show; to teach
esdevenir	to become
l'estil (*m*)	style
la façana	façade
famós	famous
ferrar	to fit with iron
la finestra	window
la guia	guidebook
la inscripció	inscription
lent	slow
la línia	line, route
el metro	underground railway
modificar	to modify, alter
mundialment	the world over
nou	new
el pintor	painter
el pla	plan, design
posar	to put, place
prendre	to take
el préssec	peach
el projecte	project
pujar	to go up, take up, get on
el quilo	kilo(gramme)
ràpid	fast
el segell	stamp
sentir	to feel; to hear
la taronja	orange
el tomàquet	tomato
la torre	tower; villa
tot	all; everything
únic	unique
el viatge	journey
visitar	to visit
el xec	cheque

Social phrases 4

Ho sento	I am sorry
No hi fa res	It doesn't matter
Passi-ho bé	Goodbye

Reading passage 5

El temple de la Sagrada Família, encara inacabat, és l'obra
principal de Gaudí. Gaudí va començar a dirigir el projecte l'any
1891, uns quants anys després del començament de les obres. En va
modificar el pla i hi va donar l'estil únic que ha esdevingut famós
mundialment.

A la façana nova hi ha una inscripció que diu «El que estàs fent
fes-ho de pressa», això en un edifici que es construeix des de més de
cent anys!

Translate the above passage into English.

Exercise 17

Make a request appropriate to the following prompts.

Example: You want three stamps.
          Doni'm tres segells si us plau.

1 You want a kilo of peaches.
2 You want to be shown where the cathedral is.
3 You want somebody to shut the window.
4 You want to be told when the museum opens.
5 You want somebody to change a cheque.
6 You want somebody to come back at four o'clock.

Exercise 18

Give the Catalan for:

1 Give me a kilo of peaches.
2 Anything else?
3 Yes, give me four oranges as well.
4 Tell him what I have done.
5 Tell him also that I have to work on Saturdays.
6 I don't understand what you are saying.
7 Would you please speak more slowly?
8 Would you please open the window?
9 I cannot open it.
10 Excuse me, is there a lift in this building?

CONVERSATION

La Maria	Vols anar a Sitges el divendres que ve? *Do you want to go to Sitges next Friday?*
En Pere	No puc anar-hi el divendres. Vaig amb en Mark a la Sagrada Família. Em va dir que vol tornar a veure-la. Vol saber-ne tot. *I can't go there on Friday. I'm going with Mark to the Sagrada Família. He told me that he wants to see it again. He wants to know everything about it.* Es pot pujar en una de les torres, oi? *You can go up inside one of the towers, can't you?*
La Maria	Sí. Hi ha ascensor. *Yes. There is a lift.*
En Pere	Com es va amb metro de la plaça de Catalunya a la Sagrada Família? *How do you get by underground from the Plaça de Catalunya to the Sagrada Família?*
La Maria	Es pren la línia tres fins a Diagonal i la línia cinc. Quan anem a Sitges doncs? Pots anar-hi el dissabte? *You take line three to Diagonal and line five. So when are we going to Sitges? Can you go on Saturday?*
En Pere	No, ho sento. El dissabte haig de treballar. *No, I'm sorry. On Saturday I've got to work.*
La Maria	No hi fa res. Puc estudiar. El diumenge? *It doesn't matter. I can study. Sunday?*
En Pere	El diumenge, sí. Què vols fer a Sitges? *Sunday, yes. What do you want to do in Sitges?*
La Maria	Vull visitar el Cau Ferrat, la casa del pintor Santiago Rusiñol. *I want to visit the 'Cau Ferrat', the house of the painter Santiago Rusiñol.*

Lesson 6

43 Imperfect tense

Catalan shares with other Romance languages another tense for referring to actions in the past, the imperfect tense.

This tense is used to refer to habitual actions, in which case it may correspond to constructions with 'used to' in English:

Passàvem les vacances a Sitges.
We used to spend the holidays in Sitges.

It is also used to refer to a situation that prevailed, in which case it may correspond to 'was' plus the present participle in English:

Llegia un llibre quan va arribar.
I was reading a book when he arrived.

Passar can serve as a model for **-ar** verbs:

passava	passàvem
passaves	passàveu
passava	passaven

Llegir can serve as a model for **-ir** verbs. The infix **-eix-** does not appear in this tense:

llegia	llegíem
llegies	llegíeu
llegia	llegien

Most other verbs take the same endings as **llegir** in the imperfect tense providing one uses the stem of the first person plural of the present tense:

Escrivia una postal.
I was writing a postcard.
Vivíem a Vic.
We used to live in Vic.

Ésser has the following forms:

era	**érem**
eres	**éreu**
era	**eren**

The imperfect form of **haver** is used to construct the pluperfect tense, just as the past tense of 'to have' is used for the same purpose in English:

M'havia posat la camisa d'en Pau.
I had put on Pau's shirt.

It gives, too, an equivalent of **hi ha** to refer to a situation in the past:

Hi havia un gat negre sota la cadira.
There was a black cat under the chair.

44 Combinations of pronouns

In Lesson 5 we saw such constructions as **Vull vendre'l** and **Li vaig vendre el pis**. There may, of course, be cases where we want to use both a direct object pronoun and an indirect object pronoun:

En Pau me'l va vendre.
Pau sold me it.

As we see, the pronouns may fuse together. This is often the case. The form that the numerous permutations take is somewhat complex. To help in this, there follow some principles with examples.

The first thing to note is that the indirect object pronoun generally comes before the direct object pronoun, as in English:

La dona me l'ha donat.
The woman has given me it.

As this example shows, **em**, **et** and **es** become **me**, **te** and **se** when they are followed by another pronoun. The direct object pronoun is more likely to lose its vowel than is the indirect object pronoun. The vowel of **en** is also very vulnerable:

La dona no me'n va parlar.
The woman did not talk to me about it.

Ja se n'havia queixat.
She had already complained about it.
Se'n va ara mateix.
She is leaving right now.

Given that the direct object pronoun is more likely to lose its vowel and that the direct object pronoun generally comes second, one can formulate another guideline, namely that an apostrophe tends towards the right-hand side of a combination.

The pronouns **ho** and **hi**, on the other hand, never lose their vowel and so when they occur together with another pronoun any loss of vowel affects that other pronoun. **Li**, however, is equally robust:

En Pau m'ho va dir.	Pau told me it.
No li ho va dir.	He did not tell him/her.
N'hi ha molts.	There are many of them.

An added complication is that when the indirect object pronoun **li** is followed by the third person pronouns **el**, **la**, **els** and **les**, the **li** commonly takes the form **hi** and comes after the direct object:

Els hi vaig donar.
I gave him them.

When two pronouns are suffixed to an infinitive, etc. both are linked to it and to each other by a hyphen or, if a vowel has been elided, by an apostrophe:

En Pau no vol dir-li-ho.
Pau doesn't want to tell him/her it.
No vol parlar-li'n.
He doesn't want to talk to him/her about it.
Vols anar-te'n?
Do you want to leave?
Posi-me'n dos quilos.
Give me two kilos (of them).

A table of the principal combinations of pronouns is given at the end of the book.

45 Possessive adjectives and pronouns

In Catalan the possessive adjective is accompanied by the definite article:

el meu marit   my husband
les teves filles   your daughters

Meu takes the following forms:

	masculine	feminine
singular	**meu**	**meva**
plural	**meus**	**meves**

Teu and **seu** follow the same pattern. **El seu** relates to the third person and so can mean 'his', 'her', 'its', 'their' and, when referring to one or more people who would be addressed as **vostè**, 'your'.

El nostre means 'our' and has the following forms:

	masculine	feminine
singular	**nostre**	**nostra**
plural	**nostres**	**nostres**

El vostre is used in respect of two or more people with whom the speaker is on informal terms. Its forms follow the same pattern as **el nostre**.

There are cases where the possessive adjective follows the noun and no definite article is used, e.g.:

Vaig trobar un amic meu.
I met a friend of mine.
Va venir a casa meva.
He came to my house.

In the first sentence the sense requires the indefinite article instead and in the second sentence the phrase is a variant of **a casa** which has no article.

Catalans may not always feel it necessary to use a possessive adjective where we do, e.g. with parts of the body. If it is felt necessary to make clear the person concerned this will generally be done with an indirect object pronoun:

M'havia tallat la mà.
I had cut my hand.

The possessive adjectives can also serve as pronouns, i.e. be used without a noun:

Deixa'm el teu llibre; he perdut el meu.
Lend me your book; I've lost mine.

46 Suffixes

Catalan may use a suffix to indicate a variation on a concept. The diminutive suffix **-et** (masculine), **-eta** (feminine), for example, may be used to refer to a smaller version of something; thus a younger brother may be referred to as a **germanet**, a teaspoon as a **cullereta**.

When applied to a person, this diminutive suffix may imply familiarity or affection rather than smaller size or younger age; thus **Joanet** is an equivalent to 'Johnny'.

A suffix may indicate a different type of the object concerned. Thus, while a **tauleta** refers to a small table, **taulell** refers to a counter or a bar.

Vocabulary 11

anar-se'n	to go away, leave
la **butxaca**	pocket
la **cadira**	chair
el **cambrer**	waiter
cantar	to sing
la **cuina**	kitchen; cuisine, cooking
la **cullera**	spoon
la **cullereta**	teaspoon
deixar	to let; to lend
el **gat**	cat
el **germà**	brother
la **germana**	sister
els **germans**	brothers; brothers and sisters
ja	already
ja no	no longer
el **llibre**	book
el **marit**	husband
mirar	to look at

morir	to die
portar	to carry; to bring; to wear
quan	when
(a) sobre	on
el **suc**	juice
tallar	to cut; interrupt
el **tallat**	small coffee
la **taula**	table
el **taulell**	counter, bar
la **tauleta de nit**	bedside table
la **televisió**	television
mirar la televisió	to watch television
les **vacances**	holidays
estar de vacances	to be on holiday

Reading passage 6

La dona cantava quan vaig arribar a casa seva. Hi havia un gat blanc a sobre la taula. Hi havia moltes taronges a la cuina. Me'n va donar quatre. Tenia cent pessetes a la butxaca. Les hi vaig donar. Hi anava els dimarts. La meva dona llegia un diari quan vaig tornar. No volia parlar-li'n. Vaig pujar a la meva habitació. Vaig posar les taronges a sobre la tauleta de nit.

Translate the above passage into English.

Exercise 19

Rewrite the following sentences substituting the appropriate pronoun for the words in brackets.

Example: La dona vol donar-me (el llibre).
La dona vol donar-me'l.

1 La dona em va donar (les flors).
2 La dona vol ensenyar-nos (la seva casa).
3 Li vaig vendre (el pis).
4 Vull queixar-me (del vi).
5 Em donaven (el diari).
6 El cambrer ens va portar (el tallat i el suc de taronja).

Exercise 20

Give the Catalan for:

1 My sister used to go to the beach on Sundays.
2 Pere bought the car in Girona.
3 My wife and I were watching television when our daughter came back.
4 I complained about our room.
5 The doctor has lost his keys.
6 My husband used to live in London.
7 Pere and Mercè gave me their cat.
8 How old was your (*formal singular*) dog when it died?
9 What are your (*informal singular*) sisters called?
10 Our children did it after coming back.

47 Passive voice

The passive voice is constructed with the appropriate tense of **ésser**, which often appears as **ser**, and a past participle:

L'edifici va ser construït l'any 1893.
The building was constructed in 1893.

The participle agrees with the noun to which it refers:

Aquestes cases van ser construïdes abans de la guerra.
These houses were built before the war.

When an agent is used to tell us who or what did the action that agent is introduced by **per** or **de**:

Gaudí va ser envestit per un tramvia.
Gaudí was struck by a tram.

Catalan often uses a reflexive construction where the passive is used in English:

Aquí es venen segells.   Stamps are sold here.

48 Prepositions 'per' and 'per a'

We have seen that the preposition **per** can equate to English 'for':

Gràcies per la postal.   Thank you for the postcard.

But 'for' can also be represented by **per a** in Catalan:

Vull comprar una postal per a la meva mare.
I want to buy a postcard for my mother.

The distinction largely reflects that between 'por' and 'para' in Spanish.

● **Per** is used, for example, to refer to the cause of an action or where exchange is involved:

Pel temps que feia no hi vaig anar.
Due to the weather I didn't go there.
Li vaig donar cent pessetes per les taronges.
I gave her a hundred pesetas for the oranges.

It is used, too, in expressions of time:

Em va deixar el llibre per una setmana.
He/she lent me the book for a week.

As we have seen, **per** may also correspond to 'through', 'by', etc.:

Van sortir pel jardí. They went out through the garden.
La casa va ser construïda per Gaudí.
The house was built by Gaudí.

● **Per a** is often associated with the idea of destination:

La casa va ser construïda per a Güell.
The house was built for Güell.

● **Per**, then, tends to relate to motive, **per a** to objective. Thus in the first of the following sentences the girl is the cause of the action, while in the second she is the beneficiary:

Ho vaig fer per la nena.
Ho vaig fer per a la nena.

Catalan usage differs from Spanish usage in that Catalan uses **per** as an equivalent of '(in order) to':

Vaig anar a Lleida per comprar una cadira.
I went to Lleida to buy a chair.

49 Ordinal numbers

The first ten ordinal numbers are as follows:

first	**primer**
second	**segon**
third	**tercer**
fourth	**quart**
fifth	**cinquè**
sixth	**sisè**
seventh	**setè**
eighth	**vuitè**
ninth	**novè**
tenth	**desè**

The ordinal numbers are adjectives and so agree with the nouns to which they refer:

Hi vaig anar per primera vegada abans-d'ahir.
I went there for the first time the day before yesterday.

50 Asking for directions

If you want to be told the way to, for example, a cathedral you can simply ask the following:

Perdoni, on és la catedral?
Excuse me, where is the cathedral?

Alternatively you can ask:

Per anar a la catedral?
How do I get to the cathedral?

In reply the phrases **tot recte** or **tot dret** might be used:

Segueixi tot recte fins a la plaça.
Continue straight on as far as the square.

If you are to turn to the left or right, you might receive instructions like the following:

Prengui el segon carrer a l'esquerra.
Take the second street on the left.
Tombi/Giri a la dreta.
Turn to the right.

Vocabulary 12

abans (de)	before
abans-d'ahir	the day before yesterday
ahir	yesterday
l'artista (*m/f*)	artist
baixar	to go down, take down, get off
captivar	to captivate
la ceràmica	ceramics
la col.lecció	collection
com que	as, since
dret	straight
a la dreta	to the right
envestir	to attack, charge
l'escriptor (*m*) } l'escriptora (*f*)	writer
a l'esquerra	to the left
l'estiu (*m*)	summer
el ferro forjat	wrought iron
girar	to turn
instal.lar	to install
l'intel.lectual (*m/f*)	intellectual
el lloc	place
la llum	light
la mare	mother
només	only
la novel.la	novel
el pare	father
els pares	parents
la primavera	spring
recte	straight
la reunió	meeting
seguir (*)	to follow, continue
el temps	time [general], weather
tombar	to turn
el tramvia	tram
traslladar(-se)	to move
la vegada	time [occasion]
el vidre	glass

(*) The verb **seguir** inserts **-eix-**.

Social phrases 5

Li/Et presento . . .   May I introduce . . .?
Molt de gust.   Pleased to meet you.
Encantat/Encantada.

Reading passage 7

El Cau Ferrat és la casa del pintor i escriptor Santiago Rusiñol.
L'any 1891, captivat per la llum de Sitges, Rusiñol s'hi va
traslladar. Dos anys després va construir el Cau Ferrat al costat del
mar. Hi va instal.lar la seva col.lecció de ferros forjats, ceràmica,
vidre, etc. El Cau Ferrat va esdevenir lloc de reunió d'artistes i
d'intel.lectuals.

És tancat els dilluns. L'entrada és dues-centes pessetes.

Answer the following questions:

1 What was the profession of Santiago Rusiñol?
2 Why did he move to Sitges?
3 Where in Sitges did he build the 'Cau Ferrat'?
4 What had he collected?
5 Can one see the collection on Mondays?

Exercise 21

Give the English for:

1 Tombi a l'esquerra.
2 Giri a la dreta.
3 Segueixi tot recte fins al mar.
4 Prengui el tercer carrer a la dreta.
5 El museu és a mà esquerra.
6 És al costat de la catedral

Exercise 22

Give the Catalan for:

1 I like reading.
2 I have just read a Catalan novel.
3 It was written by Mercè Rodoreda.
4 Her work was interrupted by the Civil War.

5 As he knows that I like reading Catalan books, my brother had given me it.
6 He had bought it in Barcelona.
7 He goes there to sell cars.
8 He went there three times in the spring.

CONVERSATION

La Maria	Hola, Pau. Fa molt de temps que no et veig. *Hello, Pau. It's a long time since I've seen you.* [a en Pere] Aquest és un amic meu. Estudia també anglès. *[to Pere] This is a friend of mine. He is also studying English.*
En Pere	Molt de gust. *Pleased to meet you.*
La Maria	Què fas aquí? *What are you doing here?*
En Pau	Els meus pares tenen un pis aquí. De jove passava tres setmanes aquí a l'estiu. Ara vinc només per uns quants dies. *My parents have a flat here. When I was young I used to spend three weeks here in the summer. Now I only come for a few days.*
La Maria	Com que coneixes Sitges, saps on és el Cau Ferrat? *As you know Sitges, do you know where the 'Cau Ferrat' is?*
En Pau	Sí. Baixeu per aquest carrer fins al capdavall i tombeu a l'esquerra. Pugeu a l'església. És una mica més enllà, a mà dreta. *Yes. Go down this street to the bottom and turn to the left. Go up to the church. It's a little bit further on, on the right-hand side.*
La Maria	Gràcies. Adéu. *Thanks. Goodbye.*
En Pau	Adéu. *Goodbye.*

Lesson 7

51 Future tense

We have seen various ways of referring to actions that took place in the past. Now we start to look forward in time.

When looking at the past tense we saw the following sentence:

El nen va menjar el plàtan.
The boy ate the banana.

If we simply add the preposition **a** between **va** and **menjar** we have completely changed the tense, the sentence now referring to the future, it corresponding to the English construction 'is going to':

El nen va a menjar el plàtan.
The boy is going to eat the banana.

In this case we use in every person the verb **anar**:

Anem a prendre el pròxim tren.
We are going to take the next train.

Another way of referring to actions in the future is formed by adding an ending to the infinitive:

Comprarem el pis.
We will buy the flat.

The endings for the different persons are as follows:

compraré	comprarem
compraràs	comprareu
comprarà	compraran

Using this tense is made easier by the fact that this set of endings is used for all verbs. Some verbs, however, add these endings to a modified form of the infinitive. Verbs that end in **-re** lose the **e** in the process:

Prendrem el tren.
We will take the train.

Some verbs change somewhat more:

aniré	I will go	**seré**	I will be
faré	I will do	**tindré**	I will have
podré	I will be able	**vindré**	I will come
sabré	I will know	**voldré**	I will want

The future tense of **haver** is **hauré**, etc.:

Ho hauré fet demà.
I will have done it tomorrow.
Hi haurà molta gent.
There will be many people there.

52 Conditional tense

A related tense is the conditional tense. As its name suggests, it is
used when carrying out the action is dependent on some condition
applying:

Hi aniríem demà però haig de treballar.
We would go there tomorrow but I have to work.
Ho faria si sabia fer-ho.
I would do it if I knew how to do it.

It is used when looking forward from some point in the past:

Vam dir que hi aniríem.
We said that we would go there.

It may be used, too, to express a desire:

Voldríem fer-ho avui.
We would like to do it today.

In each of these examples the English sentence contains the word
'would'. 'Would', then, is a good indicator of the conditional tense.
One should, however, be aware of cases where 'would' is used in
the context of a habitual action in the past and so corresponds to
the imperfect tense:

Hi anava els diumenges al matí.
He would go there on Sunday mornings.

The endings for the conditional tense are as follows:

compraria	compraríem
compraries	compraríeu
compraria	comprarien

Here, too, there is only one set of endings and it is added to the infinitive, sometimes modified as with the future tense.

53 Months

The months of the year are as follows:

January	**gener**
February	**febrer**
March	**març**
April	**abril**
May	**maig**
June	**juny**
July	**juliol**
August	**agost**
September	**setembre**
October	**octubre**
November	**novembre**
December	**desembre**

54 Dates

Now that we have the months, we can refer to dates. This is made easier by the fact that we only need cardinal numbers:

El vint-i-tres d'abril les parelles catalanes es donen llibres i roses.
On the twenty-third of April Catalan couples give each other books and roses.

Note that when the year is referred to the preposition **de** appears before the year as well as before the month:

Gaudí va morir el 7 de juny de 1926.
Gaudí died on the seventh of June 1926.

Vocabulary 13

cada	each, every
a casa	at home
el compte	bill
la gent	people
el lavabo	toilet
mateix	same; itself, etc.
jo mateix	I myself
el mercat	market
pagar	to pay (for)
la parella	couple
pintar	to paint
pròxim	next
la rosa	rose
trucar (a)	to call, ring, knock

Reading passage 8

Volia pintar la cuina però haig de treballar cada dia. El meu fill ho
va fer fa deu anys, però ja no viu a casa. Viu amb el seu germà a
França. Aquesta vegada vaig trucar a un pintor. Va dir que ho feria
el vint-i-cinc de maig. Va venir el tres de juny i no ho va fer bé.
Me'n vaig queixar. No he pagat el seu compte. Pintaré el lavabo jo
mateix.

Translate the above passage into English.

Exercise 23

*Using the prompt words construct sentences that begin with 'Va dir que
...'*

Example: arrive tomorrow.   Va dir que arribaria demà.

1 buy our flat
2 go to the market
3 write us a letter
4 do it on Monday
5 come at seven o'clock
6 lend me the book

55 Strong pronouns

The object pronouns have a different form when they are used together with a preposition:

Els meus amics parlaven de mi.
My friends were talking about me.
Aquestes roses són per a tu.
These roses are for you.
Vam sopar amb ella.
We had dinner with her.

The first person singular pronoun is **mi**. Otherwise, the strong object pronoun is the same as the subject pronoun:

mi	**nosaltres**
tu	**vosaltres**
ell	**ells**
ella	**elles**
vostè	**vostès**

There is also a third person reflexive pronoun **si**:

El meu amic va comprar un regal per a si.
My friend bought a present for himself.

These strong pronouns may be used for emphasis:

(A mi) em fa fàstic.
I hate it.

Idioms 1

We have seen that a phrase may be used as an alternative to an adverb, that, for example, 'quickly' may be translated by **de pressa** as well as by **ràpidament**.

In any language a concept may be represented by a phrase that may not be translatable word for word into another language. Thus the phrase has to be learnt as a unit. As an example, the Catalan equivalent of 'more and more', 'increasingly', is **cada cop més** or **cada vegada més**:

Bec cada cop més cafè.
I am drinking more and more coffee.

De cop is 'suddenly' and **a vegades** or **de vegades** is 'sometimes':

A vegades prenc un conyac amb el cafè.
Sometimes I have a brandy with the coffee.

Vocabulary 14

l'all (*m*)	garlic
l'allioli (*m*)	garlic and oil dressing
l'ampolla (*f*)	bottle
anar a peu	to walk, go on foot
l'arròs (*m*)	rice
el cafè	coffee
la carn	meat
la ceba	onion
el conyac	brandy
el cop	blow, strike
la crema	cream, custard
dinar	to have lunch
l'ensalada (*f*)	salad
el formatge	cheese
incloure	to include
els macarrons	macaroni
el meló	melon
l'oli (*m*)	oil
l'ou (*m*)	egg
el pa	bread
el pollastre	chicken
les postres	dessert
el regal	present
la salsa	sauce; dressing
la sopa	soup
sopar	to have dinner
típicament	typically
tradicional	traditional
triar	to choose
la vedella	calf; veal
el xai	lamb

Reading passage 9

La cuina catalana és típicament mediterrània. Es mengen la carn de xai i la de vedella, el pollastre i el peix. Es mengen els macarrons i l'arròs, les cebes, els tomàquets i els alls. L'allioli és una salsa d'all. Les postres tradicionals inclouen la crema catalana.

Answer the following questions:

1 What kinds of meat are included in Catalan cooking?
2 How is 'allioli' described?
3 At which course might one order 'crema catalana'?

Exercise 24

Give the Catalan for:

1 I want to go to the market.
2 I want to buy meat.
3 Lamb is more and more expensive.
4 Sometimes I buy chicken.
5 Jordi is going to go to the market on Friday.
6 He wants to buy a present for his mother.
7 I would like to go there with him, but I must buy the meat today.
8 I will also buy bread, cheese and eggs.
9 I would have lunch with a friend of mine but she is on holiday.
10 I will walk there and come back by bus.

CONVERSATION

En Pere   Tens gana?
             Are you hungry?

La Maria   Sí, de cop tinc gana.
             Yes, suddenly I am hungry.

El cambrer Han triat?
             Have you chosen?

En Pere   Crec que sí. De primer la sopa de peix per a mi
             i el meló per a ella. Què vols de segon?
             I think so. To begin with the fish soup for me and

the melon for her. What do you want for the main course?

La Maria   Prenc el pollastre.
I'll have the chicken.

En Pere   El pollastre per a mi també.
The chicken for me as well.

El cambrer   Ensalada?
Salad?

En Pere   Sí.
Yes.

El cambrer   I per beure?
And to drink?

En Pere   Una ampolla de vi blanc, si us plau.
A bottle of white wine, please.

Lesson 8

56 Subjunctive

We have seen sentences such as **Vull vendre'l**. In this case the person doing the wanting and the person doing the selling are one and the same. Where, however, different people are involved a subordinate clause with a special form of the verb is required:

Vull que el meu fill el vengui.
I want my son to sell it.

This special form of the verb is known as the subjunctive and is generally used in connection with a hypothetical situation. Similarly, in English we might say 'If I were rich, I would . . .', using a special form of the verb in connection with a hypothetical situation. This special form of the verb is rare in English but in the Romance languages it is common.

● The subjunctive is, then, used where there is a possibility that the situation concerned may not come about:

No crec que tornin.
I do not think that they will come back.

● It is used to express wishes, to make requests and to give orders:

Vull que reservi una habitació.
I want him/her to book a room.
Li fa res que vinguem demà?
Would you mind if we came tomorrow?
Demana-li que pugi les maletes a l'habitació.
Ask him to take the suitcases up to the room.

● It may be used when one is allowing or forbidding:

Deixeu que els nens passin.
Let the children pass.

● It is used with waiting:

Espero que arribi el meu marit.
I am waiting for my husband to arrive.

● It is used in expressions of evaluation:

Val més que hi vagis.
You had better go there.

● The subjunctive is used in connection with indeterminate situations, situations in which such forms as 'whatever', 'whoever', 'somebody who', might be used in English:

Fes el que vulguis.
Do what(ever) you want.
Busco algú que pugui ajudar-me.
I am looking for somebody who can help me.
Vull comprar-lo, per car que sigui.
I want to buy it, however expensive it may be.

● Compare the following two sentences:

No vull casar-me amb ell encara que és molt ric.
I don't want to marry him even though he is very rich.
No vull casar-me amb ell encara que sigui molt ric.
I don't want to marry him even though he may be very rich.

In the first case the indicative mood is used because the man's wealth is an established fact. In the second case the subjunctive mood is used to convey the idea of 'whether or not he is rich'. The use of the word 'may' in English is, then, another indicator that the subjunctive should perhaps be used in the Catalan equivalent.

● Other conjunctions that are or may be accompanied by the subjunctive include **abans que, així que, com si, fins que, perquè** and **sense que**:

Vull rentar-me abans que arribi el meu fill.
I want to wash before my son arrives.
Podem seure al jardí fins que arribi.
We can sit in the garden until he arrives.

The forms of the subjunctive in the present tense are as follows for **-ar** verbs:

torni	**tornem**
tornis	**torneu**
torni	**tornin**

Verbs that end in **-ir** differ in the first and second persons plural, ending in **im** and **iu**:

Vol que llegim el llibre.
He/she wants us to read the book.

In the other persons the **-ir** verbs have the infix **-eix-** where appropriate:

Vol que llegeixis el llibre.
He/she wants you to read the book.

Verbs that end in **c** in the first person singular of the present indicative take **gu** in the subjunctive:

No pots impedir que vinguin?
Can't you stop them coming?

The following are irregular verbs that take a different form:

ésser	–	**sigui**	**veure**	–	**vegi**
fer	–	**faci**	**voler**	–	**vulgui**
haver	–	**hagi**			

In the case of **anar** the stem varies:

vagi, vagis, vagi, anem, aneu, vagin

These irregular verbs take the same endings as **tornar**. In the case of **saber**, however, the endings are also irregular:

sàpiga, sàpigues, sàpiga, sapiguem, sapigueu, sàpiguen

When the situation referred to is set in the past the imperfect subjunctive is used:

Volíem que tornessin.
We wanted them to come back.

The imperfect subjunctive of **tornar** is as follows:

tornés	**tornéssim**
tornessis	**tornéssiu**
tornés	**tornessin**

Verbs that end in **-ir** replace the **e** of the ending by **i**. In this tense the **-eix-** infix is not used.

The imperfect subjunctive of **ésser** is as follows:

fos, fossis, fos, fóssim, fóssiu, fossin

Vocabulary 15

abans (que)	before
l'aeroport (*m*)	airport
així que	as soon as
ajudar	to help
algú	somebody
la **bossa**	bag
buscar	to look for; to fetch
casar-se (amb)	to marry
com si	as though, as if
demanar	to ask (for), request
encara que	even though, although
esperar	to wait; to hope
l'estona (*f*)	while
fins (que)	until
la **foto**	photo
impedir	to prevent
lliure	free, unoccupied
la **maleta**	suitcase
el **plàstic**	plastic
el **preu**	price
reconèixer	to recognise
reservar	to reserve, book
sense (que)	without
seure	to sit, be sitting
les **ulleres de sol**	sunglasses
últim	last

Exercise 25

Using the prompt words and a third person singular subject in the subsidiary clause, construct sentences that begin with 'Vull que . . .'

Example: read the book.   Vull que llegeixi el llibre.

1 give me the key
2 do it today
3 bring me the bill
4 come tomorrow
5 go away
6 tell me the price

Exercise 26

Give the Catalan for:

1 I will go to the airport tomorrow.
2 Jordi rang me a while ago to ask me to go there.
3 Do we have a room free?
4 I will give him Pere's room until Pere returns.
5 We will come back quickly.
6 He said that he is carrying only a plastic bag.
7 We will have dinner as soon as you arrive.
8 The last time he was wearing sunglasses as though he were famous.
9 Do you want me to lend you a photo so that you can recognise him?

57 'Tal', 'tan' and 'tant'

● **Tal** is used with a noun to mean 'such (a)':

No havien vist tal cosa.
They had not seen such a thing.

Together with **com** or **qual** it means '(just) as':

Ho vaig fer tal com ho volien.
I did it just as they wanted.

● **Tan** is used with an adjective to mean 'so' or 'such a':

Aquest cotxe és tan car.　This car is so expensive.
Pots comprar un cotxe tan car?
Can you buy such an expensive car?

● **Tant** means 'so much' or 'so many':

Menges sovint tant?　Do you often eat so much?
Menges sovint tant gelat?
Do you often eat so much ice cream?
Saps per què hi ha tants policies a la plaça?
Do you know why there are so many policemen in the square?

● **Tan** and **tant** are also used together with **com** to express comparison:

En Jaume és tan alt com el seu pare.
Jaume is as tall as his father.
Té tants diners com tu.
He has as much money as you.

Tant ... com ... can also translate 'both ... and ...':

Tant en Jaume com el seu pare saben fer-ho.
Both Jaume and his father know how to do it.

Idioms 2

Idioms using **tant** include the following:

tant de bo que	if only
per tant	so, therefore
de tant en tant	from time to time

Tant de bo que vingui avui!
If only he/she would come today!
Venia de tant en tant.
He/she used to come from time to time.

The second of these is one of a number of idiomatic phrases that are repetitive; other examples are:

a més a més	moreover, in addition
de mica en mica	gradually
a poc a poc	slowly

Vocabulary 16

Anglaterra	England
el **creient**	believer
els **diners**	money
durar	to last
enllaçar(-se)	to connect
l'**esperit** (*m*)	spirit
l'**estació** (*f*)	station
el **gelat**	ice cream
Itàlia	Italy
el **monestir**	monastery
el **policia**	policeman
el **refugi**	refuge, sanctuary
el **segle**	century
la **serra**	mountain range
serrat	serrated
sovint	often
tal	such (a)
tan	so, such a
tant	so much, so many
el **telefèric**	cable car
terminar	to end, finish
el/la **turista**	tourist
la **verge**	virgin

Reading passage 10

Fa molts segles que el monestir de Montserrat és un lloc sagrat dels catalans, que és el refugi de l'esperit català. Cada dia molta gent, tant creients com turistes, puja a la serra serrada per veure la Verge negra.

Translate the above passage into English.

Exercise 27

Give the Catalan for:

1 Four years ago I went to Italy three times.
2 In addition I spent a month in England.
3 If only I could travel so much every year!
4 My brother travels a lot, but I am not as rich as him.

5 From time to time I spend a few days in the Pyrenees.
6 Next month I will spend a week at a friend's in the north of Mallorca.
7 For a long time he has wanted me to go there.
8 I will come back before my holidays end so that I can paint the kitchen.

CONVERSATION

En Pere   Quin tren va a Montserrat?
Which train goes to Montserrat?

El dependent   El que va cap a Manresa.
The one that goes to Manresa.

En Pere   On s'enllaça amb el telefèric?
Where does it connect with the cable car?

El dependent   A l'estació Aeri de Montserrat.
At the station Aeri de Montserrat.

En Pere   Quant dura el viatge?
How long does the journey take?

El dependent   Una hora.
An hour.

En Pere   A quina hora surt el pròxim tren?
When does the next train leave?

El dependent   A les onze i deu.
At ten past eleven.

Reading practice

New words occurring in the following extracts are incorporated in the vocabulary list at the end of the book. The answers to the questions are given in the Key to the exercises.

When you come to read the literary extracts (16–18) for the first time, try not to refer to the English translation on the facing page. Then go through the text again, taking note of any new constructions and vocabulary, and check against the translation.

Reading passage 11

Part of an article from the newspaper 'Avui'

Més de 100.000 passatgers passaran avui dissabte per les instal.lacions de l'aeroport de Son Sant Joan, a Mallorca. Aquesta serà la primera vegada en la història de l'aeroport de Mallorca que se superarà aquesta xifra en un sol dia.

Segons ha informat la direcció de l'aeroport, durant aquest cap de setmana es produirà un moviment de 260.000 passatgers, amb més de 1.600 vols. Aquestes xifres suposen un increment del 5 per cent en relació amb el mateix cap de setmana del 1992.

L'excel.lent temporada turística i l'alta ocupació que registren els hotels de Mallorca provoquen que se superin tots els rècords que fins ara s'havien aconseguit a l'aeroport mallorquí.

Així, per tant, cada mig segon un passatger utilitzarà les instal.lacions de l'aeroport i cada 97 segons es produirà un moviment d'algun avió, d'enlairament o bé d'aterratge.

Superar la xifra de 100.000 passatgers en un sol dia significa un rècord històric, ja que la xifra més alta de passatgers a Son Sant Joan en un únic dia es va aconseguir l'1 d'agost del 1992, amb 92.000 passatgers.

Pel que fa a la nacionalitat d'origen dels visitants, el percentatge més alt són els alemanys, amb un 34,5 per cent; a continuació, els anglesos, amb el 21,3 per cent; i en tercer lloc, els espanyols, amb el 17,6 per cent.

Answer the following questions:

1 What record is about to be broken at the airport?
2 How did the number of passengers at the weekend compare with that for the same weekend in 1992?
3 To what is this development attributed?
4 Which country produced the largest number of passengers?

Reading passage 12

Part of an article from the newspaper 'Avui'

El recorregut del Barcelona Bus Turístic (L-100) permet que cada persona es pugui organitzar la visita a la ciutat d'acord amb les seves preferències a través d'un itinerari amb 15 parades situades en llocs d'interès artístic, monumental o de lleure.

El bitllet del viatge d'aquest servei és de tipus forfait i permet a l'usuari escollir la part de l'itinerari que més li interessa i realitzar-lo tantes vegades com vulgui. El passatger pot baixar i pujar del bus tantes vegades com desitgi, tenint en compte l'horari de pas dels autobusos.

El preu del bitllet per a adults és de 1.000 ptes per a tot el dia i de 700 ptes per a nens entre 4 i dotze anys. També hi ha la possibilitat de gaudir d'una tarifa especial de mig dia a partir de les 14.00 hores, amb un cost de 700 ptes.

D'altra banda, TMB ha incorporat aquesta temporada un nou vehicle a la circulació de la línia, així que ja són vuit els autobusos que funcionen cada dia amb una freqüència de pas de 15 minuts aproximadament.

També aquest mateix any s'ha procedit a la posada en marxa de dos autobusos de pis baix per tal de facilitar la utilització del servei a les persones amb problemes de mobilitat. El pas d'aquests autobusos especials per la parada de plaça Catalunya coincideix amb les hores en punt.

Answer the following questions:

1 How many journeys can a passenger make with a ticket for the tourist bus?
2 How can an adult use the service for only 700 pesetas?
3 How does the service accommodate people with mobility problems?

Reading passage 13

Article from the newspaper 'Avui'

Jordi Molins Correa, de vuit anys, i la seva germana Montse, de sis, que dimecres a la tarda van desaparèixer després de sortir d'un col.legi públic de Lleida, van passar la nit al domicili del seu company de classe Salvador Vilalta, de deu anys, segons que va informar ahir la policia.

Segons la versió policíaca, dimecres, a quarts de sis de la tarda, Salvador Vilalta va convidar els germans a jugar a casa seva, ja que els seus pares eren fora. Quan els pares de Salvador van tornar, aquest no va voler que el descobrissin jugant amb altres nens i per això va obligar Jordi i Montse a amargar-se sota el llit de la seva habitació, on van passar la nit.

L'endemà de bon matí, quan els pares de Salvador Vilalta van tornar a sortir de casa, els tres nens, en lloc d'anar a l'escola, es van dirigir als afores de la ciutat, concretament a una torre abandonada, on van ser localitzats per uns veïns que estaven assabentats de la seva desaparició.

La policia es va presentar al lloc indicat pels veïns i, quan intentava agafar el nens, Salvador Vilalta va fugir, però una hora més tard va ser localitzat. Els dos germans, que van ser trobats en estat de salut perfecte, eren buscats per la ciutat i la seva rodalia des de dimecres a la tarda.

Answer the following questions:

1 How old was Jordi Molins Correa?
2 When did Jordi and his sister disappear?
3 Where did they spend the night?
4 Why had Salvador forced Jordi and his sister to hide under his bed?
5 Where did the children go the following day?
6 Who found them?

Reading passage 14

Advertisement in magazine

COM APROFITAR FINS A L'ÚLTIMA GOTA D'AIGUA.

La col·laboració de tots els ciutadans per evitar o retardar les restriccions d'aigua és vital.
Si tots seguim aquests fàcils consells, n'estalviarem fins a un 20%.

1. Dutxa ràpida en lloc de bany.

2. Tanca l'aixeta mentre et neteges les dents, t'ensabones o t'afaites.

3. Posa la rentadora o el rentaplats només quan estiguin totalment plens.

4. Utilitza el «water» per a la seva funció, no com a cendrer o paperera.

5. Repara urgentement les aixetes o cisternes que gotegin.

6. Rega les plantes amb la màxima moderació.

Gràcies per no malgastar ni una gota d'aigua.

Àrea metropolitana de Barcelona
Medi ambient
Entitat metropolitana de serveis hidràulics
i tractament de residus

Aigües de Barcelona

Answer the following questions:

1 Should one use a shower or a bath?
2 What should one do when brushing one's teeth?
3 When should one put on the dishwasher?

Reading passage 15

Aquest any cal extremar les precaucions, no serveix de res pensar que ja som prou lluny dels arbres, creure que el jardí de casa és un lloc segur, confiar que aquest matoll sec no pot ser origen de cap incendi o estar convençuts de ser capaços de controlar la crema de rostolls.

Aquest any, aquest estiu, el perill d'incendi és màxim.

Qualsevol flama o espurna, per petita que sigui, pot tenir conseqüències devastadores; per això, si us plau, aquest estiu no enceneu foc, enlloc.

Students with a knowledge of Spanish might find it useful to note a few features which distinguish Catalan words from Spanish words. In many ways Catalan has remained closer to Latin than Spanish has. Thus Catalan retains initial **cl**, **fl** and **pl** where these have become **ll** in Spanish, e.g. Catalan **flama**, Spanish 'llama'. Catalan does not share the vowel shift of Spanish, e.g. Catalan **foc**, Spanish 'fuego'. As this last example shows, Catalan does, however, lose the masculine suffix. Catalan also loses final **n**, e.g. Catalan **jardí**, Spanish 'jardín'. The sound represented in Spanish by **ñ** is represented by **ny** in Catalan, e.g. Catalan **any**, Spanish 'año'.

Reading passage 16

From the novel 'La plaça del Diamant' (1962) by Mercè Rodoreda

Li vaig dir que m'agradava molt i ell em va dir que els ocells
negres, encara que fossin merlots, la seva mare sempre li havia dit
que portaven desgràcia. Totes les altres vegades que amb en
Quimet ens havíem trobat, després del primer dia a la plaça del
Diamant, la primera cosa que em preguntava, tirant el cap i el cos
endavant, era si ja havia renyit amb en Pere. I aquell dia no m'ho
preguntava i jo no sabia de quina manera començar a dir-li que ja
havia dit a en Pere que, amb mi, no podia ser. I em sabia molt greu
d'haver-li-ho dit, perquè en Pere s'havia quedat com un llumí
quan, després d'haver-lo encès, el bufen. I quan pensava que havia
renyit amb en Pere sentia una pena per dintre i la pena em feia
adonar que havia fet una mala acció. Segur: perquè jo, que de
dintre sempre havia estat molt natural, quan em recordava de la
cara que havia fet en Pere, sentia la pena dolenta molt endins, com
si al mig de la meva pau d'abans s'obrís una porteta que tancava un
niu d'escorpins i els escorpins sortissin a barrejar-se amb la pena i a
fer-la punxent i a escampar-se'm per la sang a fer-la negra. Perquè
en Pere, amb la veu escanyada i les nines dels ulls amb el color
entelat que li tremolava, em va dir que li havia desfet la vida. Que
l'havia convertit en una mica de fang de no-res. I va ser tot mirant
el merlot que en Quimet va començar a parlar del senyor Gaudí,
que el seu pare l'havia conegut el dia que el va aixafar el tramvia,
que el seu pare havia estat un dels que l'havien dut a l'hospital,
pobre senyor Gaudí tan bona persona, ves quina mort més de
misèria ... I que al món no hi havia res com el Parc Güell i com la
Sagrada Família i la Pedrera. Jo li vaig dir que, tot plegat, massa
ondes i massa punxes. Em va donar un cop al genoll amb el cantell
de la mà que em va fer anar la cama enlaire de sorpresa i em va dir
que si volia ser la seva dona havia de començar per trobar bé tot el
que ell trobava bé. Va fer-me un gran sermó sobre l'home i la dona
i els drets de l'un i els drets de l'altre i quan el vaig poder tallar vaig
preguntar-li:

– I si una cosa no m'agrada de cap de les maneres?

– T'ha d'agradar, perquè tu no hi entens.

I told him that I liked it a lot and he told me that his mother had
always said that black birds, even if they were blackbirds, brought
bad luck. All the other times that we had met after the first day in
the Plaça del Diamant the first thing that Quimet would ask me,
drawing his head and body forward, was whether I had fallen out
with Pere yet. And that day he did not ask me and I did not know
how to begin to tell him that I had already told Pere that there
could be nothing between us. And I was very sorry for having said
it to him because Pere had taken it like a match which, having been
lit, is blown out. And when I thought about having fallen out with
Pere I felt a pain inside and that pain made me realise that I had
done a bad thing. Without a doubt, because I, who had inside
always been very much at ease, whenever I remembered the face
that Pere had made I felt the severe pain deep inside as though in
the middle of my previous peace there had opened a small door
which enclosed a nest of scorpions and the scorpions were coming
out to blend with the pain and to make it sting, to spread it
through my blood and make it black. For Pere, with his choked
voice and the pupils of his eyes misted over, trembling, told me
that I had ruined his life. That I had turned him into a useless
lump of mud. And, looking at the blackbird, Quimet began to talk
about Mr. Gaudí, saying that his father had met him the day that
the tram knocked him down, that his father had been one of those
who had taken him to the hospital, poor Mr. Gaudí, such a good
person, what a miserable death . . . And that there was nothing in
the world like the Parc Güell and like the Sagrada Família and the
Pedrera. I said to him that there were too many curves and too
many pinnacles. He hit me on the knee with the edge of his hand
which made my leg shoot up with the shock and he said that if I
wanted to be his woman I had to start by liking everything that he
liked. He gave me a great sermon about men and women and the
rights of the one and the rights of the other and when I managed to
interrupt him I asked:

'And if I do not like something at all?'

'You have to like it, because you do not understand.'

Reading passage 17

*From the short story 'La rebel.lió de les coses' by Pere Calders,
published in 1978 in the collection 'Invasió subtil i altres contes'*

Si hagués estat possible d'investigar el fenomen des del seu origen,
s'hauria vist que tot va començar amb una vaga dels panys i dels
interruptors. Les portes no s'obrien o no es tancaven, ocasionant
alarmes que prenien de seguida unes proporcions difícils de
controlar. Els interruptors semblava que obeïssin una consigna
d'arbitrarietat, ja que a vegades deixaven engegat o encès un aparell
i d'altres es negaven a posar-lo en marxa.

Els fets es produïen escalonadament, com si algú volgués regular
malignament els períodes de tensió i els paroxismes. Les plomes
estilogràfiques abocaven el contingut de tinta al simple contacte
amb el paper, o bé es buidaven a les butxaques i els documents
gairebé sortien de les carteres buscant àvidament la taca. Cada una
d'aquestes contingències, ella tota sola, hauria ocasionat les
diminutes tragèdies ja conegudes de tothom. Però per acumulació,
el dia de la revolta de les coses es convertí[1] en una catàstrofe que
amenaçava la supervivència humana.

Pels carrers, es veien ciutadans asseguts a les voreres, amb la roba
pengim-penjam perquè els botons, els cinyells i les tires elàstiques
que subjectaven les peces al cos declinaven de sobte la seva
funcionalitat i oferien carn rosada a l'escàndol públic. Les sabates
es descordaven d'improvís i eren causa de caigudes; la proximitat
del granit i del ciment exposava els cranis a topades de molta
conseqüència. De tant en tant, algú sortia al balcó amb un posat
d'estupor i les mans plenes de molles i d'engranatges, perquè havia
provat de donar corda a un rellotge o servir-se d'un electrodomèstic
i la màquina se l'hi havia desfet materialment als dits. Grups
d'automobilistes vagaven d'esma amb el volant sota l'aixella i la
mirada perduda, a peu, molt allunyats de la prosopopeia
motoritzada. Els encenedors i els llumins van fallar tots alhora, i els
fumadors (que pretenien de fer front a la crisi encenent un cigarett)
tenien l'aire d'una extremada indefensió.

1: '... es convertí en ...' This is an example of the simple past tense
which may be found in more formal texts. The more usual form
would be '... es va convertir en ...'.

If it had been possible to investigate the phenomenon from the outset one would have seen that it all started with a strike by locks and switches. Doors wouldn't open or wouldn't close, causing anxiety that immediately assumed such proportions that it was difficult to control. Switches seemed to obey an order to be arbitrary as they sometimes left a machine switched on and sometimes refused to get it going.

Events took place at intervals as though somebody wanted to maliciously regulate the periods of tension and the outbursts. Fountain pens would discharge their ink as soon as they touched the paper or would even empty themselves in pockets, and documents would almost come out of briefcases in an avid quest for the blot. Any one of these events would, by itself, have resulted in the minor upsets experienced by everybody. But taken as a whole the day of the rebellion of the things became a catastrophe which threatened human survival.

On the streets one saw people sitting on the pavement with their clothes in disarray because the buttons, belts and elastic that held the items to the body would suddenly deny their function and expose pink flesh to public outrage. Shoes would untie themselves unexpectedly and were the cause of falls; the proximity of granite and concrete would expose skulls to serious blows. Occasionally somebody would come out onto the balcony with a look of amazement, their hands full of springs and cogs because they had tried to wind up a clock or use some domestic appliance, the machine having literally dismantled itself in their hands. Groups of motorists wandered around semi-consciously with their steering wheel under their arm and with a distant gaze, on foot, far removed from their motorised upstart. Lighters and matches ceased to work all at the same time and smokers (who wished to confront the crisis by lighting a cigarette) looked utterly helpless.

Reading passage 18

From the novel 'Cames de seda' (1992) by Maria Mercè Roca

Amb el cotxe s'han enfilat amunt pels carrers costeruts i deserts. La majoria de les cases són tancades i ofereixen un aspecte abandonat. La seva és en un carrer molt estret on totes les cases són antigues. L'entrada queda a mà dreta; és una casa de dos pisos, amb graons al davant de la porta i dues grans finestres de mig arc a banda i banda. La façana és bruta i les persianes de dalt haurien de canviar-se; la porta, vermella, està una mica despintada. A la paret, entre la porta i la finestra de la dreta hi ha unes lletres de ferro negre, rodones, que diuen Vil.la Feliç. La Feliça, en deien, quan hi passaven totes les vacances i els caps de setmana llargs. L'Adriana mira la façana i no diu res. Cada vegada hi ve menys: a l'Albert la platja no li agrada i la Clara no hi ha acabat de trobar una colla d'amics al seu gust. Per a qui serà, la Feliça? A ella la casa que de veritat li agrada és l'altra, petita i blanca, amb el jardí al davant i els gats que es passegen amunt i avall del mur. Aquella més que aquesta, pensa, i en canvi és aquesta que potser serà meva un dia. Les cases són com les persones, pensa: les estimes o no les estimes i no hi ha res a fer. Aparco aquí?, pregunta la Roser. Vaig a buscar les claus, diu l'Adriana, i surt del cotxe i camina carrer amunt i s'atura al davant d'una casa petita. Truca. L'obre una noia molt jove que la mira fixament però no li diu res.

– Sóc l'Adriana, de la Feliça; no em coneixes? És que ens hem deixat les claus. Saps on les guarda, la teva àvia?

La noia no fa cap gest d'interès, no somriu, continua escrutant-la amb una mirada impertinent. No ho sé, diu al final, i afegeix: però ho puc mirar. I se'n va cap a dins i la deixa al pas de la porta, esperant. L'Adriana bufa, malhumorada. Al cap d'un moment la noia apareix amb una clau de ferro, antiga, lligada a un clauer de macramé descolorit i desfilat que la Clara havia fet quan era petita.

– És això?

– Sí, gràcies. No hi estarem gaire – se li acut, per no haver de tornar-la a veure –: Per no molestar-te un altre cop quan marxem, la deixaré a la bústia.

They have worked their way up in the car through the steep and deserted streets. Most of the houses are closed up and have a deserted look. Hers is a very narrow street in which all the houses are old. The gate is on the right-hand side; it is a two-storey house with steps in front of the door and two big semi-arched windows side by side. The façade is dirty and the upstairs blinds need changing; the door, red, is flaking somewhat. On the wall, between the door and the right-hand window, there are some black iron letters, round ones, which say Vil.la Feliç. La Feliça, they called it when they used to spend all the holidays and the long weekends there. Adriana looks at the façade and says nothing. She comes here less and less; Albert doesn't like the beach and Clara has not managed to find a group of friends to her liking. Who will it be for, La Feliça? The house that she really likes is the other one, the small white one with the garden in front and the cats that walk up and down the wall. That one more than this one, she thinks, and yet it is this one that will perhaps be mine some day. Houses are like people, she thinks; you either love them or you don't and there is nothing that you can do about it.

'Shall I park here?', Roser asks. 'I'm going to get the keys', says Adriana and gets out of the car, walks up the street and stops in front of a little house. She rings. It is opened by a very young girl who stares at her and says nothing.

'I am Adriana, from La Feliça. Do you not know me? We have left the keys here. Do you know where she keeps them, your grandmother?'

The girl shows no sign of interest, doesn't smile, keeps on studying her with an impertinent gaze. 'I don't know', she says at last and adds 'but I can look.' And she goes inside and leaves her on the doorstep, waiting. Adriana pants impatiently. After a while the girl appears with an old iron key held by a keyring of discoloured macramé that Clara had made when she was little.

'Is this it?'

'Yes, thank you. We won't be there much', she thinks to add so as not to have to see her again. 'So that I don't bother you again when we leave I'll put it in the letterbox.'

Key to Exercises

LESSON 1

Exercise 1: 1 Un home vell. 2 Una dona rica. 3 Una dona jove.
4 Un home català. 5 Una ciutat catalana. 6 El barri vell.
7 L'església vella. 8 Aquella casa groga. 9 La primera casa.
10 Aquesta casa blanca. 11 El vi blanc. 12 La Costa Brava.

Reading passage 1: 1 Yes. 2 At the top of the Rambla.

Exercise 2: 1 El fill de l'home vell és professor. 2 La casa del
professor és al capdavall del carrer. 3 És groga. 4 El cotxe del
professor és blanc. 5 La dona vella és mes rica que el professor.
6 És la dona més rica de la ciutat. 7 La casa de la (dona) vella és a
la plaça. 8 La casa és blanca. 9 És molt gran. 10 És prop de
l'església principal. 11 L'església és molt vella. 12 És més vella
que el palau.

LESSON 2

Exercise 3: 1 Sis ciutats catalanes. 2 Pels carrers estrets del Barri
Gòtic. 3 Unes dones riques del barri. 4 Els carrers amples de
l'Eixample. 5 Les esglésies blanques. 6 Els despatxos de la caixa.
7 Les botigues a la plaça. 8 Les habitacions del pis. 9 Aquells dos
pisos. 10 Tres autobusos vermells. 11 Quatre taxis negres i grocs.
12 Els fills del professor.

Reading passage 2: 1 It is the widest street of the 'Eixample'.
2 The Casa Batlló and the Pedrera. 3 Gaudí.

Exercise 4: 1 és. 2 és. 3 està. 4 està. 5 és. 6 és.

Exercise 5: 1 El senyor Puig treballa en una sucursal de la Caixa de
Sabadell al passeig de Gràcia. 2 En Jaume és periodista.
3 L'Antoni no és periodista. 4 És professor. 5 En Jaume i
l'Antoni estan contents perquè no treballen avui. 6 Juguen a
futbol. 7 La Maria estudia anglès. 8 Ella i una amiga passegen fins
a la plaça de Catalunya. 9 La Maria menja un plàtan. 10 L'amiga
de la Maria no menja res.

LESSON 3

Reading passage 3: 1 At the sea. 2 Newspapers, flowers and birds. 3 At the top of the Rambla, near the Plaça de Catalunya. 4 One will remain in Barcelona for ever more.

Exercise 6: 1 Vull jugar a futbol. 2 Vull menjar peix. 3 La dona no vol menjar res. 4 Tinc mal de cap. 5 No, visc a Manchester. 6 Treballo en una botiga.

Exercise 7: 1 El senyor Puig viu en un pis al carrer Pau Claris. 2 El pis té cinc habitacions. 3 El senyor Puig té tres fills i una filla. 4 La filla es diu Maria. 5 Estudia anglès a la Universitat de Barcelona. 6 Com es diu el professor? 7 Es diu Brian Mott. 8 És de Londres però viu a Barcelona des de l'any 1972.

Exercise 8: 1 L'home va rentar el cotxe. 2 En Joan va beure el vi. 3 Vas anar al mar? 4 Van jugar a futbol? 5 Vam vendre el pis. 6 El metge va tancar la porta.

Exercise 9: 1 Són les cinc i vint. 2 Són les cinc menys deu. 3 És un quart de dues. 4 Es tanca a dos quarts de dues. 5 Comença cap a les vuit. 6 Arriba a les deu i deu del matí.

Exercise 10: 1 En Pere i la Maria van al cinema. 2 A quina hora comença la pel.lícula? 3 Comença a les vuit. 4 Es troben a la plaça a tres quarts de vuit. 5 A quina hora es tanca la caixa? 6 És oberta des de les nou fins a les dues. 7 Quants anys té en Mark? 8 Té vint anys. 9 Es va llevar a dos quarts de deu. 10 Qui va rentar la camisa? 11 La nena (jove) no vol rentar-se. 12 L'home que va vendre el pis viu a Sitges.

LESSON 4

Exercise 11: 1 L'home llegeix un diari. 2 No vol obrir la porta. 3 Em va veure amb la Maria davant la catedral. 4 La Maria em va escriure una carta en anglès. 5 Vaig llegir la carta a l'autobús. 6 Em va dir el que vol fer demà passat. 7 Vol anar al museu al parc. 8 A quina hora s'obre el museu? 9 Crec que s'obre a les deu. 10 No vull anar al museu.

Reading passage 4: 1 On the north side. 2 The mountains and the sea. 3 It is drier.

Exercise 12: 1 M'agrada el vi negre. 2 No m'agrada la cervesa. 3 M'agrada molt viatjar. 4 No m'agraden gens els plàtans.

5 M'agrada molt aquest pis. 6 No m'agrada jugar a tennis.

Exercise 13: 1 És tres mil sis-centes pessetes. 2 És tres-centes cinquanta pessetes. 3 És quaranta-cinc pessetes. 4 És dos mil cinc-centes pessetes. 5 És dos mil sis-centes cinquanta pessetes. 6 Són quatre-centes vuitanta pessetes.

Exercise 14: 1 Què et sembla el vi negre? 2 No m'agrada gens el vi negre. 3 M'agrada més/M'estimo més/Prefereixo el vi blanc. 4 T'agrada beure (la) cervesa? 5 Sí, m'agrada molt la cervesa. 6 Bec molta cervesa. 7 T'agrada viure a Barcelona? 8 Sí, però m'agrada passar els caps de setmana a Sitges. 9 Tinc un pis a Sitges des de l'any 1990. 10 Tinc allà una amiga que es dependenta. 11 Té vint-i-sis anys. 12 Ens agrada passar unes quantes hores a la platja.

LESSON 5

Exercise 15: 1 La nena no vol menjar-los. 2 Els he perdut. 3 No puc obrir-la. 4 No vull parlar-ne. 5 Vull donar-li les flors. 6 Vaig escriure-li.

Exercise 16: 1 Acabo de comprar una camisa. 2 M'agrada també aquesta però no vull comprar-la. 3 Quantes camises tens? 4 En tinc moltes. 5 Sap(s) si hi ha una farmàcia prop d'aquí? 6 Ha(s) vist la Maria? 7 Sí, la vaig veure a la platja. 8 Li ha(s) donat el diari? 9 No, vull tornar a llegir-lo. 10 Sé que vol fer-ho demà. 11 Però no puc anar-hi demà. 12 Haig de treballar a l'hotel fins a les set.

Reading passage 5: The church of the Holy Family, still unfinished, is the principal work of Gaudí. Gaudí began to direct the project in 1891, a few years after the work was begun. He modified the plan and gave it the unique style that has become famous around the world.

On the new façade there is an inscription which says 'Whatever you are doing do it quickly', this on a building which they have been constructing for more than a hundred years!

Exercise 17: 1 Posi'm/Doni'm un quilo de préssecs. 2 Ensenyi'm on és la catedral. 3 Tanqui la finestra. 4 Digui'm a quina hora s'obre el museu. 5 Canvi aquest xec. 6 Torni a les quatre. More politely, one can add 'si us plau' or use such constructions as 'Pot tancar la finestra?', 'Li fa res tancar la finestra?'

Exercise 18: 1 Posi'm/Doni'm un quilo de préssecs. 2 Alguna cosa més? 3 Sí, posi'm/doni'm també quatre taronges. 4 Digui-li el que he fet. 5 Digui-li també que haig de treballar els dissabtes. 6 No entenc el que diu (vostè). 7 Pot parlar mes lentament? 8 Pot obrir la finestra? 9 No puc obrir-la. 10 Perdoni, hi ha (un) ascensor en aquest edifici?

LESSON 6

Reading passage 6: The woman was singing when I arrived at her house. There was a white cat on the table. There were many oranges in the kitchen. She gave me four of them. I had a hundred pesetas in my pocket. I gave her them. I used to go there on Tuesdays. My wife was reading a newspaper when I came back. I didn't want to talk to her about it. I went up to my room. I put the oranges on the bedside table.

Exercise 19: 1 La dona me les va donar. 2 La dona vol ensenyar-nos-la. 3 El hi vaig vendre. 4 Vull queixar-me'n. 5 Me'l donaven. 6 El cambrer ens els va portar.

Exercise 20: 1 La meva germana anava a la platja els diumenges. 2 En Pere va comprar el cotxe a Girona. 3 La meva dona i jo miravem la televisió quan va tornar la nostra filla. 4 Vaig queixar-me de la nostra habitació. 5 El metge ha perdut les seves claus. 6 El meu marit vivia a Londres. 7 En Pere i la Mercè em van donar el seu gat. 8 Quants anys tenia el seu gos quan va morir? 9 Com es diuen les teves germanes? 10 Els nostres fills ho van fer després de tornar.

Reading passage 7: 1 He was a painter and writer. 2 Because he was captivated by the light. 3 Beside the sea. 4 Wrought iron, ceramics, glass, etc. 5 No; it is closed.

Exercise 21: 1 Turn to the left. 2 Turn to the right. 3 Continue straight ahead as far as the sea. 4 Take the third street on the right. 5 The museum is on the left-hand side. 6 It is beside the cathedral.

Exercise 22: 1 M'agrada llegir. 2 Acabo de llegir una novel.la catalana. 3 Va ser escrita per Mercè Rodoreda. 4 La seva obra va ser tallada per la guerra civil. 5 Com que sap que m'agrada llegir (els) llibres catalans, el meu germà me l'havia donat. 6 L'havia comprat a Barcelona. 7 Hi va per vendre cotxes. 8 Hi va anar tres vegades a la primavera.

LESSON 7

Reading passage 8: I wanted to paint the kitchen but I have to work every day. My son did it ten years ago but he does not live at home any more. He lives with his brother in France. This time I called a painter. He said that he would do it on the twenty-fifth of May. He came on the third of June and he did not do it well. I complained (about it). I have not paid his bill. I will paint the toilet myself.

Exercise 23: 1 Va dir que compraria el nostre pis. 2 Va dir que aniria al mercat. 3 Va dir que ens escriuria una carta. 4 Va dir que ho faria el dilluns. 5 Va dir que vindria a les set. 6 Va dir que em deixaria el llibre.

Reading passage 9: 1 Lamb and veal. 2 Garlic dressing. 3 Sweet course.

Exercise 24: 1 Vull anar al mercat. 2 Vull comprar carn. 3 El xai és cada cop més car. 4 De/A vegades compro pollastre. 5 En Jordi anirà al mercat (el) divendres. 6 Vol comprar un regal per a la seva mare. 7 Voldria anar-hi amb ell, però haig de comprar la carn avui. 8 Compraré també pa, formatge i ous. 9 Dinaria amb una amiga meva però està de vacances. 10 Hi aniré a peu i tornaré amb autobús.

LESSON 8

Exercise 25: 1 Vull que em doni la clau. 2 Vull que ho faci avui. 3 Vull que em porti el compte. 4 Vull que vingui demà. 5 Vull que se'n vagi. 6 Vull que em digui el preu.

Exercise 26: 1 Aniré demà a l'aeroport. 2 En Jordi em va trucar fa una estona per demanar-me que hi vagi. 3 Tenim una habitació lliure? 4 Li donaré l'habitació d'en Pere fins que torni en Pere. 5 Tornarem de pressa. 6 Va dir que porta només una bossa de plàstic. 7 Soparem així que arribeu. 8 L'última vegada portava ulleres de sol com si fos famós. 9 Vols que et deixi una foto perquè puguis reconèixer-lo?

Reading passage 10: For many centuries the monastery of Montserrat has been a sacred place for the Catalans, has been the refuge of the Catalan spirit. Every day many people, both believers and tourists, go up to the serrated mountain range to see the Black Virgin.

Exercise 27: 1 Fa quatre anys vaig anar tres vegades a Itàlia. 2 A més a més vaig passar un mes a Anglaterra. 3 Tant de bo que pugui viatjar tant cada any! 4 El meu germà viatja molt, però (jo) no sóc tan ric com ell. 5 De tant en tant passo uns quants dies als Pirineus. 6 El mes que ve passaré una setmana a ca un amic al nord de Mallorca. 7 Fa molt de temps que vol que hi vagi. 8 Tornaré abans que terminin/s'acabin les meves vacances perquè pugui pintar la cuina.

Reading passage 11: 1 For the first time more than 100,000 passengers are about to pass through the airport in a single day. 2 It was 5% higher. 3 The excellent tourist season and the high hotel occupancy. 4 Germany.

Reading passage 12: 1 As many as he wants. 2 By travelling after 2 p.m. 3 The service has two buses with a low floor.

Reading passage 13: 1 Jordi was eight years old. 2 They disappeared on Wednesday afternoon. 3 They spent it at the home of their classmate Salvador. 4 He did not want his parents to find him playing with other children. 5 They went to a deserted villa on the outskirts of the town. 6 They were found by some neighbours.

Reading passage 14: 1 One should use a shower. 2 One should turn off the tap. 3 One should only put it on when it is completely full.

Appendix

Irregular verbs

This section gives a few forms of a number of the more common irregular verbs.

	Present indicative (1st and 3rd, singular and plural)	Present subjunctive (1st and 3rd, singular)	Perfect (1st singular)
anar:	vaig, va anem, van	vagi	he anat
beure:	bec, beu bevem, beuen	begui	he begut
caure:	caic, cau caiem, cauen	caigui	he caigut
conèixer:	conec, coneix coneixem, coneixen	conegui	he conegut
creure:	crec, creu creiem, creuen	cregui	he cregut
deure:	dec, deu devem, deuen	degui	he degut
dir:	dic, diu diem, diuen	digui	he dit
escriure:	escric, escriu escrivim, escriuen	escrigui	he escrit
ésser:	sóc, és som, són	sigui	he estat
estar:	estic, està estem, estan	estigui	he estat
fer:	faig, fa fem, fan	faci	he fet
haver:	he (haig), ha hem, han	hagi	he hagut
obrir:	obro, obre obrim, obren	obri	he obert
poder:	puc, pot podem, poden	pugui	he pogut

prendre:	prenc, pren prenem, prenen	prengui	he pres
rebre:	rebo, rep rebem, reben	rebi	he rebut
riure:	ric, riu riem, riuen	rigui	he rigut
saber:	sé, sap sabem, saben	sàpiga	he sabut
sortir:	surto, surt sortim, surten	surti	he sortit
tenir:	tinc, té tenim, tenen	tingui	he tingut
vendre:	venc, ven venem, venen	vengui	he venut
venir:	vinc, ve venim, vénen	vingui	he vingut
veure:	veig, veu veiem, veuen	vegi	he vist
viure:	visc, viu vivim, viuen	visqui	he viscut
voler:	vull, vol volem, volen	vulgui	he volgut

Combinations of pronouns

These tables indicate how indirect and direct pronouns combine when they are used together.

The following table gives the combinations when the pronouns precede the verb:

Indirect objects	Direct objects								
	el	la	l'	els	les	ho	hi	en	n'
em	me'l	me la	me l'	me'ls	me les	m'ho	m'hi	me'n	me n'
et	te'l	te la	te l'	te'ls	te les	t'ho	t'hi	te'n	te n'
es	se'l	se la	se l'	se'ls	se les	s'ho	s'hi	se'n	se n'
li	el hi	la hi	li l'	els hi	les hi	li ho	li hi	li'n	li n'

The indirect objects 'els' and 'ens' do not fuse with direct objects.

The following table gives the combinations when the pronouns come after the verb:

Indirect objects	Direct objects						
	-lo	-la	-los	-les	ho	hi	-ne/'n
-me	-me'l	-me-la	-me'ls	-me-les	-m'ho	-m'hi	-me'n
-te	-te'l	-te-la	-te'ls	-te-les	-t'ho	-t'hi	-te'n
-se	-se'l	-se-la	-se'ls	-se-les	-s'ho	-s'hi	-se'n
-li	-l'hi	-la-hi	-los-hi	-les-hi	-li-ho	-li-hi	-li'n
-nos	-nos-el	-nos-la	-nos-els	-nos-les	-nos-ho	-nos-hi	-nos-en
-los	-los-el	-los-la	-los-els	-los-les	-los-ho	-los-hi	-los-en

Examples:

En Pau m'ho va dir.	Pau told me (it).
Els hi vaig donar.	I gave them to him/her.
No vull parlar-li'n.	I don't want to talk to him/her about it.

Mini-dictionary

(*f*) feminine (*m*) masculine (*pl*) plural

Catalan–English

a to, at, in
abans (de) before
abans-d'ahir the day before
  yesterday
abril April
acabar to finish, complete
acabar de to have just
l'accident (*m*) accident
aconseguir to achieve
adéu goodbye
adonar-se to realise
l'aeroport (*m*) airport
afaitar(-se) to shave
afegir to add
els **afores** outskirts
agafar to seize, catch
agost August
agradar to please
ahir yesterday
l'aigua (*f*) water
aixafar to crush
l'aixella (*f*) armpit
l'aixeta (*f*) tap
així thus, in this way
així que as soon as
això this, that
  per això consequently
ajudar to help
l'ajuntament (*m*) town council;
  town hall
alemany German
algú somebody
algun some, any
alhora at the same time
l'all (*m*) garlic
allà there
l'allioli (*m*) garlic and oil
  dressing

alt tall, high
altre other
amagar(-se) to hide
amb with; (transport) by
amenaçar to threaten
l'amic (*m*) friend (*m*)
l'amiga (*f*) friend (*f*)
ample wide
l'ampolla (*f*) bottle
anar to go
anar-se'n to go away, leave
Anglaterra England
anglès English
antic old
l'any (*m*) year
aparcar to park
aparèixer to appear
aquell that
aquest this
aquí here
ara now
l'arbre (*m*) tree
l'arribada (*f*) arrival
arribar to arrive
l'arròs (*m*) rice
l'artista (*m/f*) artist
l'ascensor (*m*) lift
assabentar (de) to inform
  (about, of)
l'assegurança (*f*) insurance
assemblar-se a to resemble
asseure's to sit down
l'aterratge (*m*) landing
aturar(-se) to stop
l'autobús (*m*) bus
l'automobilista (*m/f*) motorist
l'autopista (*f*) motorway
avall down

l'**avi** (*m*) grandfather
l'**àvia** (*f*) grandmother
l'**avió** (*m*) plane
avui today
baix low
baixar to go down, get off,
    take down
el **balcó** balcony
ballar to dance
el **banc** bank; bench
la **banda** side; tape
    d'altra banda moreover, in
    addition
el **bany** bath
el **bar** bar
la **barca** boat
barrejar to mix
el **barret** hat
el **barri** district, quarter
bé well
bell beautiful
benvingut welcome
beure to drink
la **bicicleta** bicycle
el **bitllet** ticket; banknote
el **bitllet d'anada i tornada**
    return ticket
blanc white
blau blue
bo good
el **bolígraf** ball-point pen
la **bossa** bag
la **botiga** shop
el **botó** button
brau wild, rugged
britànic British
brut dirty
bufar to blow (away)
buidar to empty
buit empty
buscar to look for; to fetch
la **bústia** letterbox
la **butxaca** pocket
cada each, every
la **cadira** chair
el **cafè** coffee; café

la **caiguda** fall
la **caixa** bank
caldre to be necessary
la **calor** heat
la **cama** leg
el **cambrer** waiter
el **camí** road, way
caminar to walk, go
la **camisa** shirt
cantar to sing
el **cantell** edge
canviar to change
el **cap** head
cap a towards; (time) at about
capac capable, able
el **capdamunt** top
el **capdavall** bottom
el **cap de setmana** weekend
car dear, expensive
la **cara** face
la **carn** meat
el **carnet de conduir** driving
    licence
el **carrer** street
la **carretera** road
la **carta** letter
la **cartera** wallet; briefcase
la **casa** house
    a casa at home
casar-se (**amb**) to marry
casat married
castellà Castilian
català Catalan
Catalunya Catalonia
la **catedral** cathedral
el **cau** den
caure to fall
la **causa** cause
la **ceba** onion
el **cendrer** ashtray
cent hundred
la **ceràmica** ceramics
la **cervesa** beer
el **cigarret** cigarette
la **cigarreta** cigarette
el **ciment** cement, concrete

cinc five
el cinema cinema
cinquanta fifty
el cinyell belt
el ciutadà citizen
la ciutat town, city
civil civil
la clau key
el clauer keyring
el coll neck; throat
la colla group
la col.lecció collection
el col.legi school
el color colour
  com how
  com que as, since
  com si as though, as if
el començament beginning
  començar to begin
el company friend, companion
  comprar to buy
el compte bill
    tenir en compte to bear in
    mind
  concretament specifically
  conduir to drive, lead
la coneguda acquaintance (*f*)
el conegut acquaintance (*m*)
  conèixer to (get to) know
el consell (piece of) advice
  construir to build
  content happy
  convidar to invite
el conyac brandy
el cop blow, strike
    cada cop més more and
    more
la copa glass
la corda string, rope
    donar corda a to wind up
el cos body
la cosa thing
la costa coast; slope
el costat side
  costerut steep
el cotó cotton

el cotxe car
el crani skull
el creient believer
la crema cream, custard
  cremar to burn
  creure to believe, think
la cuina kitchen; cuisine,
  cooking
el cuir(o) leather
la cullera spoon
la cullereta teaspoon
  dalt above, upstairs
  darrera/e (de) behind
  davant (de) in front (of)
  de of, from
  deixar to let; to lend
  demà tomorrow
  demà passat the day after
  tomorrow
  demanar to ask (for), request
la dent tooth
el dependent employee; shop
  assistant (*m*)
la dependenta employee; shop
  assistant (*f*)
  des de since, from
  desaparèixer to disappear
  descobrir to discover
  desembre December
la desgràcia misfortune, bad
  luck
  desitjar to desire, wish
el despatx office
  despertar(-se) to wake
  després (de) after
  deu ten
el dia day
el diari newspaper
el diccionari dictionary
  difícil difficult
  dijous Thursday
  dilluns Monday
  dimarts Tuesday
  dimecres Wednesday
  dinar to have lunch
els diners money

dir to say, tell
dir-se to be called
la **direcció** direction; management
el **director** manager
la **directora** manageress
dirigir to direct
dissabte Saturday
el **dit** finger
diumenge Sunday
divendres Friday
dolent bad
el **domicili** home
la **dona** woman; wife
donar to give
dormir to sleep
dos (*m*) two
dret straight; right
el **dret** right
dues (*f*) two
durar to last
la **dutxa** shower
l'**edifici** (*m*) building
l'**eixugamà** (*m*) towel
eixugar to wipe, dry
l'**electrodomèstic** (*m*) domestic appliance
embolicar to wrap (up)
l'**empresa** (*f*) company
emprovar to try on
en in; of it, etc.
encara still
encara que even though, although
encendre to light
l'**encenedor** (*m*) lighter
endavant forward
l'**endemà** (*m*) the following day
enfilar to thread
l'**enlairament** (*m*) take-off
enllà further
més enllà de beyond
enllaçar(-se) to connect
ensabonar to soap, to lather
l'**ensalada** (*f*) salad
ensenyar to show; to teach

entendre to understand
l'**entrada** (*f*) entrance; ticket
entrar (**a**/**en**) to enter (into)
envestir to attack, charge
enviar to send
escampar to spread
escanyar to strangle
escocès Scottish
Escòcia Scotland
l'**escola** (*f*) school
escollir to choose
l'**escriptor** (*m*) writer (*m*)
l'**escriptora** (*f*) writer (*f*)
escriure to write
esdevenir to become
l'**església** (*f*) church
l'**esma** (*f*) instinct, skill
esmorzar to have breakfast
Espanya Spain
espanyol Spanish
esperar to wait; to hope
l'**esperit** (*m*) spirit
l'**espurna** (*f*) spark
esquerre left
ésser to be
l'**est** east
l'**estació** (*f*) station; season
estalviar to save
estar to be
estendre('s) to stretch
l'**estil** (*m*) style
estimar to like, love
estimar-se més to prefer
l'**estiu** (*m*) summer
l'**estómac** (*m*) stomach
l'**estona** (*f*) while
estret narrow; tight
l'**estudiant** (*m*) student (*m*)
l'**estudianta** (*f*) student (*f*)
estudiar to study
evitar to avoid
fa . . . . . . ago
la **façana** façade
fàcil easy, simple
fallar to go wrong
la **família** family

famós famous
el fang mud
la farmàcia chemist's, pharmacy
el fàstic loathing, revulsion
febrer February
feliç happy
fer to do, make
ferrar to fit with iron
el ferro (forjat) (wrought) iron
el ferrocarril railway
la festa party; festival
el fet deed, act
el fill son
la filla daughter
els fills sons; children
la finestra window
fins (a) as far as; until
la flama flame
la flor flower
el foc fire
la font fountain; spring
fora away, outside
formar to form
el formatge cheese
la forquilla (f) fork
fosc dark
la foto(grafia) photo(graph)
França France
francès French
la frontera border, frontier
fugir to run away
el fumador smoker
fumar to smoke
funcionar to work, function
gairebé almost
la gana hunger
el ganivet knife
la gasolina petrol
la gasolinera petrol station
el gat cat
gaudir (de) to enjoy
el gel ice
el gelat ice cream
gener January
la Generalitat government of
    Catalonia

el genoll knee
la gent people
el gerent manager
el germà brother
la germana sister
els germans brothers; brothers
    and sisters
girar to turn
el gos dog
la gota drop
gotejar to drip
gòtic Gothic
gràcies thank you
gran big, large, great
la Gran Bretanya Great Britain
el graó step
groc yellow
el grup group
guardar to keep
la guerra war
la guia guidebook
el gust taste; pleasure
l'habitació (f) room
l'habitant (m/f) inhabitant
hola hello
l'home (m) man
l'hora (f) hour
l'horari (m) timetable
l'hospital (m) hospital
l'hotel (m) hotel
i and
l'illa (f) island
impedir to prevent
important important
l'incendi (m) fire
incloure to include
la inscripció inscription
intentar (de) to try (to)
l'interès (m) interest
interessant interesting
l'interruptor (m) switch
Irlanda Ireland
irlandès Irish
Itàlia Italy
ja already
ja no no longer

el **jardí** garden
jove young
jugar to play
juliol July
juny June
el **lavabo** toilet
lent slow
la **línia** line, route
llarg long
la **llauna** tin, can
llegir to read
llest clever; ready
la **llet** milk
la **lletra** letter
el **lleure** leisure
llevar to raise; to remove
llevar-se to get up
el **llibre** book
lligar to tie
el **llit** bed
la **lliura** pound
lliure free, unoccupied
el **lloc** place
llogar to hire, rent
la **llum** light
el **llumí** match
lluny (de) far (from)
Londres London
la **mà** hand
la **maduixa** strawberry
mai ever
maig May
la **majoria de** most (of)
mal bad
malalt ill
la **maleta** suitcase
malgastar to waste
la **manera** way, manner
el **mapa** map
la **màquina** machine
el **mar** sea
març March
la **mare** mother
el **marit** husband
marxar to go, leave
massa too (many)

mateix same; itself, etc.
ara mateix right now
jo mateix I myself
el **matí** morning
de bon matí early in the
morning
el **matoll** brushwood
mediterrani Mediterranean
la **meitat** half
el **meló** melon
menjar to eat
mentre while
el **menú** menu
menys less, minus
el **mercat** market
el **merlot** blackbird
el **mes** month
més more
a més a més moreover, in
addition
el **metge** doctor
el **metro** underground railway
una **mica** a little
de mica en mica gradually
mig half
el **mig** middle
mil thousand
millor better; best
la **mirada** gaze
mirar to look at
la **missa** mass
modificar to modify, alter
molestar to bother
molt much; very
el **món** world
la **moneda** currency; coin
el **monestir** monastery
morir to die
la **mort** death
mullat wet, soaked
mundialment the world over
la **muntanya** mountain
muntanyós mountainous
el **mur** wall
el **museu** museum
negre black; (of wine) red

el **nen** (young) boy
la **nena** (young) girl
net clean
netejar to clean
la **nit** night
el **niu** nest
no no; not
el **noi** lad, boy
la **noia** girl
només only
noranta ninety
el **nord** north
nou new; nine
la **novel.la** novel
novembre November
o or
obeir to obey
obert open
l'**obra** (f) work
obrir to open
l'**ocell** (m) bird
octubre October
oferir to offer, present
l'**oli** (m) oil
on where
l'**onda** (f) wave
l'**ou** (m) egg
el **pa** bread
pagar to pay (for)
el **palau** palace
el **pany** lock
el **paper** paper
la **paperera** waste-paper bin
el **paquet** packet, parcel
la **parada** bus stop
la **paraula** word
el **parc** park
el **pare** father
el **parell** pair
la **parella** couple
els **pares** parents
la **paret** wall
parlar (**de**) to speak, talk
(about)
la **part** part
el **pas** step

passar to pass, spend (time)
el **passatger** passenger
el **passeig** avenue
passejar to (go for a) walk
el **pastís** pastry, cake
la **pau** peace
la **pedra** stone
la **pedrera** quarry
el **peix** fish
la **pel.lícula** film
la **pena** pain
pengim-penjam in disarray
pensar to think
per by, through, for
perdre to lose
el **perill** danger
el, la **periodista** journalist
però but
perquè because; so that
la **persiana** blind
la **pesseta** peseta
el **peu** foot
a peu on foot
pintar to paint
el **pintor** painter
els **Pirineus** Pyrenees
el **pis** flat; storey
la **piscina** swimming pool
el **pla** plan, design
la **plaça** square
el **plànol** plan, map
la **planura** plain
el **plàstic** plastic
el **plat** plate, dish
el **plàtan** banana; plane tree
la **platja** beach
ple full
la **ploma** pen; feather
ploure to rain
la **pluja** rain
el **poble** town, village; people
pobre poor
poc little
a poc a poc slowly
poder to be able (to)
el **policia** policeman

el **pollastre** chicken
la **poma** apple
la **porta** door
  portar to carry; to bring; to wear
  posar to put, place
la **postal** postcard
les **postres** dessert
  potser maybe, perhaps
  preferir to prefer
  preguntar to ask
  prendre to take
  presentar to introduce
la **pressa** hurry
    de pressa quickly
el **préssec** peach
el **preu** price
la **primavera** spring
  primer first
  principal principal
el **professor** teacher (*m*)
la **professora** teacher (*f*)
el **projecte** project
  prop (de) near (to)
  prou sufficient(ly), enough
  provar (de) to try (to)
la **província** province
  pròxim next
  pujar to go up, get on, take up
la **punxa** point
  punxar to sting
  qualsevol any
  quan when
  quant how much
  quants how many
  quaranta forty
  quart fourth
el **quart** quarter
  quatre four
  que that
  què? what?
    per què? why?
  quedar-se to stay, remain
  queixar-se (de) to complain (about)

  qui? who?
el **quilo** kilo(gramme)
  quin? which?
  ràpid fast
el **raspall** brush
la **ratlla** stripe
la **rebaixa** discount, reduction
  reconèixer to recognise
el **record** souvenir
  recordar-se (de) to remember
el **recorregut** route
  recte straight
el **refugi** refuge, sanctuary
el **regal** present
  regar to water, irrigate
el **regne** kingdom
el **Regne Unit** United Kingdom
el **rei** king
  reial royal
el **rellotge** clock, watch
la **rentadora** washing machine
el **rentaplats** dishwasher
  rentar(-se) to wash
  renyir (amb) to quarrel (with), fall out (with)
  res anything
  reservar to reserve, book
el **restaurant** restaurant
  retardar to delay
la **reunió** meeting
la **revista** magazine
  ric rich
la **roba** clothes
  robar to steal
la **rodalia** surrounding area
  rodó round
la **rosa** rose
el **rostoll** stubble
la **sabata** shoe
  saber to know
  saber greu to regret, be sorry
el **sabó** soap
el **sacerdot** priest
  sagrat holy, sacred
la **salsa** sauce; dressing
la **salut** health

la **sang** blood
sec dry
la **seda** silk
el **segell** stamp
el **segle** century
segon second
el **segon** second
segons according to
seguir to follow, continue
segur safe; certain
seixanta sixty
semblar to seem
sempre always
sense without
sentir to feel; to hear
el **senyor** gentleman; Mr.
la **senyora** lady; Mrs.
la **serra** mountain range
serrat serrated
el **servei** service
servir to serve, be of use
servir-se de to use
set seven
la **set** thirst
setanta seventy
setembre September
la **setmana** week
seure to sit, be sitting
si if
sí yes
el **símbol** symbol
sis six
(a) **sobre** on
(de) **sobte** suddenly
el **sol** sun
somriure to smile
la **sopa** soup
sopar to have dinner
el **soroll** noise
la **sorpresa** surprise
la **sortida** exit; departure
sortir to leave, go out, depart
sota under
sovint often
el **suc** juice
la **sucursal** branch

el **sud** south
superar to exceed
la **supervivència** survival
la **taca** stain, spot, blot
tal such (a)
tallar to cut; to interrupt
el **tallat** small coffee
també also, as well
tan so, such a
tancar to close
tant so much, so many
  de tant en tant from time to time
  per tant so, therefore
tard late
la **tarda** afternoon
la **targeta de crèdit** credit card
la **taronja** orange
la **tassa** cup
la **taula** table
el **taulell** counter, bar
el **taxi** taxi
el **te** tea
el **telefèric** cable car
el **telèfon** telephone
la **televisió** television
la **temporada** season, period
el **temps** time; weather
tenir to have
el **tennis** tennis
tercer third
terminar to end, finish
la **tinta** ink
típic typical
tirar to pull, draw
tocar to touch; to play
el **tomàquet** tomato
tombar to turn
la **topada** impact, collision
tornar to return, go/come back
tornar a to ... again
la **torre** tower; villa
tot all, everything
tothom everybody
la **tovallola** towel

el **tramvia** tram
traslladar(-se) to move
treballar to work
tremolar to tremble
el **tren** train
trenta thirty
tres three
el **triangle** triangle
triar to choose
trobar to meet; to find
trucar (a) to call, ring, knock
el/la **turista** tourist
l'**ull** (*m*) eye
les **ulleres de sol** sunglasses
últim last
únic unique, only
la **universitat** university
utilitzar to use
les **vacances** holiday
la **vaga** strike
vagar to loiter, wander
la **vedella** calf; veal
la **vegada** time, occasion
    cada vegada més more and
    more
el **veí** neighbour, local resident
vell old
vendre to sell
venir to come

la **verge** virgin
la **veritat** truth
vermell red
el **vespre** evening
la **veu** voice
veure to see
el **vi** wine
el **viatge** journey
viatjar to travel
la **vida** life
el **vidre** glass
vint twenty
visitar to visit
la **vista** view
viure to live
el **vol** flight
el **volant** steering wheel
voler to want
la **vorera** pavement
vostè(s) you
vuit eight
vuitanta eighty
el **wàter** toilet
el **xai** lamb
el **xec** cheque
la **xifra** figure
xinès Chinese
la **xocolata** chocolate

English–Catalan

able capaç
   to be able (to) poder
about: at about cap a
above dalt
accident accident (*m*)
according to segons
achieve aconseguir
acquaintance conegut (*m*);
   coneguda (*f*)
act fet (*m*)
add afegir
addition: in addition d'altra banda,
   a més a més
advice consell (*m*)
after després (de)
afternoon tarda (*f*)
again una altra vegada, tornar a ...
... ago fa ...
airport aeroport (*m*)
all tot
almost gairebé
already ja
also també
alter modificar
although encara que
always sempre
and i
any algun, qualsevol
appear aparèixer
apple poma (*f*)
appliance electrodomèstic (*m*)
April abril
arm braç (*m*)
armpit aixella (*f*)
arrival arribada (*f*)
arrive arribar
artist artista (*m/f*)
as com que
as ... as tan ... com
as if com si
as soon as així que
as though com si

as well (also) també
ashtray cendrer (*m*)
ask preguntar
ask for demanar
at a, en
August agost
avenue passeig (*m*)
avoid evitar
away fora
   go away anar-se'n
   run away fugir
bad mal, dolent
bad luck desgràcia (*f*)
bag bossa (*f*)
balcony balcó (*m*)
banana plàtan (*m*)
bank banc (*m*), caixa (*f*)
banknote bitllet (*m*)
bar bar (*m*); taulell (*m*)
bath bany (*m*)
be ésser; estar
beach platja (*f*)
beautiful bell
because perquè
become esdevenir
bed llit (*m*)
beer cervesa (*f*)
before abans (de); abans que
begin començar
beginning començament (*m*)
behind darrera (de), darrere (de)
believe creure
believer creient (*m*)
belt cinyell (*m*)
bench banc (*m*)
best millor
better millor
beyond més enllà de
bicycle bicicleta (*f*)
big gran
bill compte (*m*)
bird ocell (*m*)

black negre
blackbird merlot (*m*)
blind persiana (*f*); cec
blood sang (*f*)
blot taca (*f*)
blow cop (*m*); bufar
blue blau
boat barca (*f*)
body cos (*m*)
book llibre (*m*); reservar
border frontera (*f*)
bother molestar
bottle ampolla (*f*)
bottom capdavall (*m*)
boy [young] nen (*m*); [older] noi (*m*)
branch [organisation] sucursal (*f*) [plant] branca (*f*)
brandy conyac (*m*)
bread pa (*m*)
breakfast: have breakfast esmorzar
briefcase cartera (*f*)
bring portar
British britànic
brother germà (*m*)
brush raspall (*m*)
build construir
building edifici (*m*)
burn cremar
bus autobús (*m*)
bus stop parada (*f*)
but però
button botó (*m*)
buy comprar
by per; [transport] amb
cable car telefèric (*m*)
café cafè (*m*)
cake pastis (*m*)
calf vedella (*f*)
call trucar (a)
called: to be called dir-se
can see 'able'; llauna (*f*)
capable capaç
captivate captivar
car cotxe (*m*)
carry portar

cat gat (*m*)
Catalan català
Catalonia Catalunya
catch agafar
cathedral catedral (*f*)
cause causa (*f*)
cement ciment (*m*)
century segle (*m*)
ceramics ceràmica (*f*)
certain segur
chair cadira (*f*)
change canviar
cheese formatge (*m*)
chemist's farmàcia (*f*)
cheque xec (*m*)
chicken pollastre (*m*)
Chinese xinès
chocolate xocolata (*f*)
choose escollir, triar
church església (*f*)
cigarette cigarret (*m*), cigarreta (*f*)
cinema cinema (*m*)
city ciutat (*f*)
civil civil
clean net; netejar
clever llest
clock rellotge (*m*)
close tancar
clothes roba (*f*)
coast costa (*f*)
coffee cafè (*m*), tallat (*m*)
coin moneda (*f*)
collection col.lecció (*f*)
collision topada (*f*)
colour color (*m*)
come venir
come back tornar
companion company (*m*)
company empresa (*f*)
complain (about) queixar-se (de)
complete acabar
concrete ciment (*m*)
connect enllaçar(-se)
consequently per això
continue seguir
cooking cuina (*f*)

cotton cotó (*m*)
counter taulell (*m*)
couple parella (*f*)
cream crema (*f*)
credit card targeta de crèdit (*f*)
crush aixafar
cuisine cuina (*f*)
cup tassa (*f*)
currency moneda (*f*)
custard crema (*f*)
cut tallar
dance ballar
danger perill (*m*)
dark fosc
daughter filla (*f*)
day dia (*m*)
dear car
death mort (*f*)
December desembre
deed fet (*m*)
delay retardar
depart sortir
departure sortida (*f*)
design pla (*m*); disseny (*m*)
desire desitjar
dessert postres (*fpl*)
dictionary diccionari (*m*)
die morir
difficult difícil
dinner: have dinner sopar
direct dirigir
direction direcció (*f*)
dirty brut
disappear desaparèixer
disarray: in disarray pengim-penjam
discount rebaixa (*f*)
discover descobrir
dish plat (*m*)
dishwasher rentaplats (*m*)
district barri (*m*)
do fer
doctor metge (*m*)
dog gos (*m*)
door porta (*f*)
down avall

go down, take down baixar
draw [pull] tirar; [sketch] dibuixar
dressing salsa (*f*)
drink beure; beguda (*f*)
drip gotejar
drive conduir
driving licence carnet de conduir (*m*)
drop gota (*f*)
dry sec; eixugar
each cada
east est (*m*)
easy fàcil
eat menjar
edge cantell (*m*)
egg ou (*m*)
eight vuit
eighty vuitanta
eleven onze
employee dependent (*m*); dependenta (*f*)
empty buit; buidar
end terminar
England Anglaterra
English anglès
enjoy gaudir (de)
enough prou
enter (into) entrar (a/en)
entrance entrada (*f*)
even though encara que
evening vespre (*m*)
every cada
everybody tothom
everything tot
exceed superar
excuse perdonar
exit sortida (*f*)
expensive car
eye ull (*m*)
façade façana (*f*)
face cara (*f*)
fall caure; caiguda (*f*)
fall out (with) renyir (amb)
family família (*f*)
famous famós
far (from) lluny (de)

as far as fins (a)
fast ràpid
father pare (*m*)
feather ploma (*f*)
February febrer
feel sentir
festival festa (*f*)
fetch buscar
few: a few uns quants
fifty cinquanta
figure xifra (*f*)
film pel.lícula (*f*)
find trobar
finger dit (*m*)
finish acabar, terminar
fire [general] foc (*m*);
  [conflagration] incendi (*m*)
first primer
fish peix (*m*); pescar
five cinc
flame flama (*f*)
flat pis (*m*); pla
flight vol (*m*)
flower flor (*f*)
follow seguir
foot peu (*m*)
  on foot a peu
football futbol (*m*)
for per; per a
fork forquilla (*f*)
form formar
forty quaranta
forward endavant
fountain font (*f*)
four quatre
fourth quart
France França
free lliure
French francès
Friday divendres
friend amic (*m*), amiga (*f*)
from (des) de
front: in front (of) davant (de)
frontier frontera (*f*)
full ple
function funcionar

further enllà
garden jardí (*m*)
garlic all (*m*)
gaze mirada (*f*)
gentleman senyor (*m*)
German alemany
get off baixar
get on pujar
get up llevar-se, aixecar-se
girl [young] nena (*f*); [older] noia
  (*f*)
give donar
glass [vessel] copa (*f*); [material]
  vidre (*m*)
go anar
go away anar-se'n
go back tornar
go down baixar
go out sortir
go up pujar
good bo
goodbye adéu, passi-ho bé
Gothic gòtic
gradually de mica en mica
grandfather avi (*m*)
grandmother àvia (*f*)
great gran
Great Britain Gran Bretanya (*f*)
group grup (*m*), colla (*f*)
guidebook guia (*f*)
half meitat (*f*); mig
hand mà (*f*)
happy feliç, content
hat barret (*m*)
have tenir; haver
have to haver de
head cap (*m*)
health salut (*f*)
hear sentir
heat calor (*f*)
hello hola
help ajudar
here aquí
hide amagar(-se)
high alt
hire llogar

holidays vacances (*fpl*)
holy sagrat
home domicili (*m*)
  at home a casa
hope esperar
hospital hospital (*m*)
hotel hotel (*m*)
hour hora (*f*)
house casa (*f*)
how com
how many quants
how much quant
hundred cent
hunger gana (*f*)
hurry pressa (*f*)
  be in a hurry tenir pressa
husband marit (*m*)
ice gel (*m*)
ice cream gelat (*m*)
if si
if only tant de bo que
ill malalt
impact topada (*f*)
important important
in a, en
include incloure
inform (about, of) assabentar (de)
inhabitant habitant (*m/f*)
inscription inscripció (*f*)
install instal.lar
instinct esma (*f*)
insurance assegurança (*f*)
intellectual intel.lectual (*m/f*)
interest interès (*m*)
interesting interessant
interrupt tallar
introduce presentar
invite convidar
Ireland Irlanda
Irish irlandès
iron ferro (*m*)
  wrought iron ferro forjat (*m*)
irrigate regar
island illa (*f*)
Italy Itàlia
January gener

journalist periodista (*m/f*)
journey viatge (*m*)
juice suc (*m*)
June juny
July juliol
just: have just acabar de
keep guardar
key clau (*f*)
keyring clauer (*m*)
kilogramme quilo (*m*)
king rei (*m*)
kingdom regne (*m*)
kitchen cuina (*f*)
knee genoll (*m*)
knife ganivet (*m*)
knock trucar (a)
know [fact] saber; [person, place]
  conèixer
lad noi (*m*)
lady senyora (*f*)
lamb xai (*m*)
landing aterratge (*m*)
large gran
last últim; durar
late tard
lather ensabonar
lead conduir; plom (*m*)
leather cuir(o) (*m*)
leave anar-se'n, sortir, marxar
left esquerre
  to the left a l'esquerra
leg cama (*f*)
leisure lleure (*m*)
lend deixar
less menys
let [allow] deixar; [rent] llogar
letter [communication] carta (*f*);
  [character] lletra (*f*)
letterbox bústia (*f*)
life vida (*f*)
lift ascensor (*m*); aixecar
light llum (*f*); encendre
lighter encenedor (*m*)
like estimar; com
line línia (*f*)
little petit; poc

a little una mica
live viure
loathing fàstic (*m*)
lock pany (*m*); tancar amb clau
loiter vagar
London Londres
long [size] llarg; [time] molt (de temps)
look at mirar
look for buscar
lose perdre
love estimar
low baix
lunch: have lunch dinar
machine màquina (*f*)
magazine revista (*f*)
make fer
man home (*m*)
management direcció (*f*)
manager director (*m*)
manageress directora (*f*)
manner manera (*f*)
many molts
   how many quants
   so many tants
   too many massa
map mapa (*m*), plànol (*m*)
March març
market mercat (*m*)
married casat
marry casar-se (amb)
mass missa (*f*)
match llumí (*m*)
May maig
maybe potser
meat carn (*f*)
Mediterranean mediterrani
meet trobar
meeting reunió (*f*)
melon meló (*m*)
menu menú (*m*)
middle mig (*m*)
milk llet (*m*)
million milió (*m*)
minus menys
misfortune desgràcia (*f*)

mix barrejar
modify modificar
monastery monestir (*m*)
Monday dilluns
money diners (*mpl*)
month mes (*m*)
more més
more and more cada cop més, cada vegada més
moreover d'altra banda, a més a més
morning matí (*m*)
mother mare (*f*)
motorist automobilista (*m/f*)
motorway autopista (*f*)
mountain muntanya (*f*)
mountain range serra (*f*)
mountainous muntanyós
move moure('s), traslladar(-se)
much molt
   how much quant
   so much tant
   too much massa
mud fang (*m*)
museum museu (*m*)
must: see 'have to'
narrow estret
near (to) prop (de)
necessary: to be necessary caldre
neck coll (*m*)
nest niu (*m*)
never no . . . mai
new nou
newspaper diari (*m*)
next pròxim
night nit (*f*)
nine nou
ninety noranta
no no
noise soroll (*m*)
north nord (*m*)
not no
nothing no . . . res
novel novel.la (*f*)
November novembre
now ara

right now ara mateix
obey obeir
occasion vegada (*f*)
October octubre
of de
offer oferir
office despatx (*m*)
often sovint
oil oli (*m*)
old vell, antic
on (a) sobre
one un (*m*); una (*f*)
onion ceba (*f*)
only només; únic, sol
if only tant de bo que
open obrir; obert
or o
orange taronja (*f*)
other altre
outside fora
outskirts afores (*mpl*)
packet paquet (*m*)
pain pena (*f*)
paint pintar
painter pintor (*m*)
pair parell (*m*)
palace palau (*m*)
paper paper (*m*)
parcel paquet (*m*)
parents pares (*mpl*)
park parc (*m*); aparcar
part part (*f*)
party festa (*f*)
pass passar
passenger passatger (*m*)
pastry pastís (*m*)
pavement vorera (*f*)
pay (for) pagar
peace pau (*f*)
peach préssec (*m*)
pen ploma (*f*), bolígraf (*m*)
people gent (*f*); poble (*m*)
perhaps potser
peseta pesseta (*f*)
petrol gasolina (*f*)
petrol station gasolinera (*f*)

pharmacy farmàcia (*f*)
photograph foto(grafia) (*f*)
place lloc (*m*); posar
plain planura (*f*)
plan pla (*m*); plànol (*m*)
plane avió (*m*)
plane tree plàtan (*m*)
plastic plàstic (*m*)
play [sport] jugar (a); [music] tocar
please agradar; si us plau
pleasure gust (*m*)
pocket butxaca (*f*)
point indicar; punxa (*f*)
policeman policia (*m*)
poor pobre
postcard postal (*f*)
pound lliura (*f*)
prefer estimar-se més, preferir
present regal (*m*); oferir
prevent impedir
price preu (*m*)
priest sacerdot (*m*)
principal principal
project projecte (*m*)
province província (*f*)
pull tirar
put posar
Pyrenees Pirineus (*mpl*)
quarrel (with) renyir (amb)
quarry pedrera (*f*)
quarter [fraction] quart (*m*);
[district] barri (*m*)
quickly ràpidament, de pressa
railway ferrocarril (*m*)
rain ploure; pluja (*f*)
raise llevar, aixecar
read llegir
ready llest
realise adonar-se
recognise reconèixer
red vermell, roig; [of wine] negre
reduction rebaixa (*f*)
refuge refugi (*m*)
regret saber greu
remain quedar-se
remember recordar-se de

remove llevar
rent llogar
request demanar
resemble assemblar-se a
reserve reservar
restaurant restaurant (*m*)
return tornar
return ticket bitllet d'anada i
   tornada (*m*)
revulsion fàstic (*m*)
rice arròs (*m*)
rich ric
right dret (*m*); dret
   be right tenir raó
   to the right a la dreta
ring trucar (a); anell (*m*)
road carretera (*f*), camí (*m*)
room habitació (*f*)
rope corda (*f*)
rose rosa (*f*)
round rodó
route [bus] línia (*f*), recorregut
   (*m*); [road] camí (*m*)
royal reial
rugged brau
run córrer
run away fugir
sacred sagrat
safe segur
salad ensalada (*f*)
same mateix
   at the same time alhora
sanctuary refugi (*m*)
Saturday dissabte
sauce salsa (*f*)
save estalviar
say dir
school escola (*f*), col.legi (*m*)
Scotland Escòcia
Scottish escocès
sea mar (*m*)
season estació (*f*); temporada (*f*)
second segon; segon (*m*)
see veure
seem semblar
seize agafar

sell vendre
send enviar
September setembre
serrated serrat
serve servir
service servei (*m*)
seven set
seventy setanta
shave afaitar(-se)
shirt camisa (*f*)
shoe sabata (*f*)
shop botiga (*f*)
shop assistant dependent (*m*),
   dependenta (*f*)
show ensenyar
shower [bath] dutxa (*f*); [rain]
   xàfec (*m*)
side costat (*m*), banda (*f*)
silk seda (*f*)
simple fàcil
since des de; com que
sing cantar
sister germana (*f*)
sit, be sitting seure
sit down asseure's
six sis
sixty seixanta
skill esma (*f*)
skull crani (*m*)
sleep dormir
slope costa (*f*)
slow lent
slowly lentament, a poc a poc
small petit
smile somriure
smoke fum (*m*); fumar
smoker fumador
so tan; per tant
so many tants
so much tant
so that perquè
soaked mullat
soap sabó (*m*); ensabonar
some algun; (*pl*) alguns, uns
somebody algú
sometimes a vegades, de vegades

son fill (*m*)
soon avait
  as soon as així que
sorry: be sorry sentir, saber greu
soup sopa (*f*)
south sud (*m*)
souvenir record (*m*)
Spain Espanya
Spanish espanyol
spark espurna (*f*)
speak (about) parlar (de)
specifically concretament
spend [time] passar; [money]
  despendre
spirit esperit (*m*)
spoon cullera (*f*)
spot taca (*f*)
spring [water] font (*f*); [season]
  primavera (*f*)
square plaça (*f*); quadrat
stain taca (*f*)
stamp segell (*m*)
station estació (*f*)
stay quedar-se
steal robar
steep costerut
steering wheel volant (*m*)
step [stride] pas (*m*); [stairs] graó
  ·(*m*)
still tranquil; encara
sting punxar
stomach estómac (*m*)
stone pedra (*f*)
stop aturar(-se)
  bus stop parada (*f*)
storey pis (*m*)
straight dret, recte
strawberry maduixa (*f*)
street carrer (*m*)
stretch estendre('s)
strike [blow] cop (*m*); [protest] vaga
  (*f*)
string corda (*f*)
stripe ratlla (*f*)
student estudiant (*m*), estudianta
  (*f*)

study estudiar
style estil (*m*)
such (a) tal
suddenly de cop, (de) sobte
sufficient(ly) prou
suitcase maleta (*f*)
summer estiu (*m*)
sun sol (*m*)
Sunday diumenge
sunglasses ulleres de sol (*fpl*)
sure segur
surprise sorpresa (*f*)
surrounding area rodalia (*f*)
survival supervivència (*f*)
swimming pool piscina (*f*)
switch interruptor (*m*)
symbol símbol (*m*)
table taula (*f*)
  bedside table tauleta de nit (*f*)
take prendre
take down baixar
take up pujar
take-off enlairament (*m*)
talk (about) parlar (de)
tall alt
tap aixeta (*f*)
tape banda (*f*)
taste gust (*m*)
taxi taxi (*m*)
tea te (*m*)
teach ensenyar
teacher professor (*m*), professora
  (*f*)
teaspoon cullereta (*f*)
telephone telèfon (*m*)
television televisió (*f*)
tell dir
ten deu
tennis tennis (*m*)
thank you (for) gràcies (*fpl*) (per)
that aquell; això; que
there allà, hi
therefore per tant
thing cosa (*f*)
think pensar; creure
third tercer

thirst set (*f*)
thirty trenta
this aquest; això
thousand mil
thread enfilar; fil (*m*)
threaten amenaçar
three tres
throat coll (*m*)
through per
Thursday dijous
thus així
ticket [travel] bitllet (*m*);
  [admission] entrada (*f*)
  return ticket bitllet d'anada i
  tornada (*m*)
tie lligar
tight estret
time [general] temps (*m*); [occasion]
  vegada (*f*)
  from time to time de tant en tant
timetable horari (*m*)
tin llauna (*f*)
to a
today avui
toilet lavabo (*m*), wàter (*m*)
tomato tomàquet (*m*)
tomorrow demà
  day after tomorrow demà passat
too; too much; too many massa
tooth dent (*f*)
top capdamunt (*m*)
touch tocar
tourist turista (*m/f*)
towards cap a
towel tovallola (*f*), eixugamà (*m*)
tower torre (*f*)
town ciutat (*f*), poble (*m*)
town council ajuntament (*m*)
town hall ajuntament (*m*)
traditional tradicional
train tren (*m*)
tram tramvia (*m*)
travel viatjar
tree arbre (*m*)
tremble tremolar
triangle triangle (*m*)

truth veritat (*f*)
try (to) intentar (de), provar (de)
try on emprovar
Tuesday dimarts
turn girar, tombar
twelve dotze
twenty vint
two dos (*m*), dues (*f*)
typical típic
under sota
underground railway metro (*m*)
understand entendre
unique únic
United Kingdom Regne Unit (*m*)
university universitat (*f*)
unoccupied lliure
until fins (a); fins que
upstairs dalt
use servir-se de, utilitzar
  be of use servir
veal vedella (*f*)
very molt
view vista (*f*)
villa torre (*f*)
village poble (*m*)
virgin verge (*f*)
visit visitar
voice veu (*f*)
wait esperar
waiter cambrer (*m*)
wake despertar(-se)
walk caminar, anar a peu
  go for a walk passejar
wall mur (*m*), paret (*f*)
wallet cartera (*f*)
want voler
war guerra (*f*)
wash rentar(-se)
washing machine rentadora (*f*)
waste malgastar
watch rellotge (*m*); mirar
water aigua (*f*); regar
wave onda (*f*)
way [path] camí (*m*); [manner]
  manera (*f*)
  in this way així, d'aquesta

manera
wear portar
weather temps (*m*)
Wednesday dimecres
week setmana (*f*)
weekend cap de setmana (*m*)
welcome benvingut
   you're welcome de res
well bé
wet mullat
what què; el que
when quan
where on
which quin; que
while estona (*f*); mentre
white blanc
who qui; que
why per què
wide ample
wife dona (*f*)
wild brau
wind up donar corda a
window finestra (*f*)

wine vi (*m*)
wipe eixugar
wish desitjar
with amb
without sense (que)
woman dona (*f*)
word paraula (*f*)
work obra (*f*); [employment]
   treballar; [function] funcionar
world món (*m*)
   the world over mundialment
wrap (up) embolicar
write escriure
writer escriptor (*m*), escriptora (*f*)
wrong: to go wrong fallar
year any (*m*)
yellow groc
yes sí
yesterday ahir
   day before yesterday abans-d'ahir
you vostè(s)
young jove

Index

The numbers refer to section headings.

144